MATH

Grade 6

Thomas J. Richards
Mathematics Teacher
Lamar Junior-Senior High School
Lamar, Missouri

SPECTRUM

Columbus, Ohio

Photo Credits

Larry Molmud, **2;** David Madison/Tony Stone Images,
52; Andy Stack/Tony Stone Images, **80;** Doug
Martin/SRA/McGraw-Hill, **104;** Chuck Savage/The Stock
Market, **136.**

Send all inquiries to:
School Specialty Publishing
8720 Orion Place
Columbus, OH 43240-2111

ISBN 1-57768-406-0

17 18 19 20 21 22 QPD 11 10 09 08 07 06

Contents

Readiness Check

Solve each problem.

	a	*b*	*c*	*d*
1.	63 59 +75	564 308 +97	68495 +32878	7865 9718 +4656
2.	287 −56	1360 −984	67325 −49097	84006 −8139
3.	359 ×8	697 ×10	230 ×45	68 ×97
4.	567 ×43	608 ×27	765 ×219	3568 ×794
5.	6)7248	7)5824	42)8862	88)35288
6.	90)7030	74)985	48)29314	74)59734

Readiness Check (continued)

Write each answer in simplest form.

	a	b	c	d
7.	$\dfrac{4}{7} \times \dfrac{7}{10}$	$\dfrac{5}{18} \times \dfrac{3}{10}$	$\dfrac{4}{15} \times \dfrac{5}{6}$	$3 \times \dfrac{2}{7}$
8.	$\dfrac{2}{3} \times 9$	$\dfrac{11}{18} \times 54$	$1\dfrac{2}{3} \times \dfrac{1}{6}$	$\dfrac{4}{5} \times 2\dfrac{2}{3}$
9.	$5\dfrac{1}{2} \times 4$	$12 \times 6\dfrac{3}{4}$	$1\dfrac{5}{6} \times 5\dfrac{1}{2}$	$2\dfrac{1}{2} \times 1\dfrac{1}{10}$

10.

$$\dfrac{2}{9}$$
$$+\dfrac{5}{9}$$

$$\dfrac{1}{3}$$
$$+\dfrac{2}{9}$$

$$\dfrac{1}{2}$$
$$+\dfrac{1}{6}$$

$$\dfrac{5}{12}$$
$$+\dfrac{1}{4}$$

11.

$$6$$
$$+\dfrac{7}{12}$$

$$5\dfrac{1}{2}$$
$$2\dfrac{1}{3}$$

$$4\dfrac{2}{3}$$
$$+4\dfrac{1}{5}$$

$$4\dfrac{8}{9}$$
$$+5\dfrac{1}{2}$$

12.

$$\dfrac{2}{3}$$
$$-\dfrac{1}{5}$$

$$\dfrac{3}{8}$$
$$\dfrac{1}{3}$$

$$4$$
$$-\dfrac{1}{8}$$

$$2\dfrac{3}{8}$$
$$-\dfrac{1}{4}$$

13.

$$8\dfrac{5}{6}$$
$$-2\dfrac{3}{10}$$

$$4$$
$$-2$$

$$6\dfrac{1}{4}$$
$$-2\dfrac{5}{8}$$

$$7\dfrac{1}{5}$$
$$-6\dfrac{7}{10}$$

Addition Facts (Form A)

	a	b	c	d	e	f	g	h
1.	8 +2	3 +2	6 +2	2 +8	9 +2	4 +2	1 +2	7 +1
2.	5 +4	7 +9	1 +1	6 +9	4 +3	5 +8	5 +1	2 +0
3.	2 +7	0 +0	5 +2	3 +3	9 +1	1 +4	7 +8	6 +0
4.	6 +3	3 +1	7 +7	0 +1	2 +2	6 +8	5 +7	2 +9
5.	4 +4	8 +8	1 +6	8 +3	2 +6	8 +9	0 +3	7 +6
6.	9 +3	2 +5	7 +5	4 +9	6 +7	3 +4	8 +7	3 +9
7.	5 +3	3 +8	5 +9	3 +5	9 +7	5 +6	4 +8	9 +8
8.	1 +8	9 +5	0 +4	8 +4	3 +6	7 +4	6 +6	2 +3
9.	6 +4	4 +5	7 +3	6 +5	9 +6	0 +8	4 +6	8 +6
10.	8 +5	3 +7	2 +4	9 +4	4 +7	7 +2	9 +9	5 +5

Addition Facts (Form B)

	a	b	c	d	e	f	g	h
1.	7 +2	5 +0	1 +5	8 +2	3 +2	6 +2	4 +9	2 +1
2.	8 +3	2 +9	9 +1	6 +3	4 +2	7 +0	3 +0	9 +4
3.	1 +7	7 +3	4 +8	2 +8	8 +1	1 +1	9 +9	3 +9
4.	8 +9	3 +3	0 +0	6 +9	2 +2	8 +0	3 +8	7 +7
5.	4 +3	6 +4	8 +4	5 +2	9 +2	4 +7	6 +8	1 +0
6.	7 +4	2 +3	1 +9	8 +8	0 +2	7 +6	5 +9	9 +3
7.	3 +4	9 +6	5 +3	7 +5	4 +6	8 +7	2 +7	3 +7
8.	5 +4	6 +5	0 +6	2 +4	8 +5	3 +6	7 +8	5 +8
9.	9 +8	3 +5	7 +9	4 +4	6 +6	5 +5	0 +9	2 +5
10.	5 +7	8 +6	2 +6	9 +7	5 +6	9 +5	4 +5	6 +7

Subtraction Facts (Form A)

	a	b	c	d	e	f	g	h
1.	11 −8	9 −5	10 −7	7 −6	8 −4	15 −9	9 −8	13 −7
2.	13 −4	9 −9	15 −6	7 −4	4 −2	17 −8	8 −2	10 −6
3.	14 −9	7 −2	10 −5	3 −2	2 −1	10 −8	6 −4	13 −9
4.	16 −8	6 −2	11 −3	7 −3	9 −7	11 −4	8 −5	11 −6
5.	14 −7	4 −1	12 −4	5 −4	10 −2	15 −7	8 −3	14 −8
6.	12 −3	9 −4	11 −5	7 −7	7 −5	14 −6	8 −0	12 −5
7.	11 −7	6 −0	17 −9	5 −2	0 −0	13 −8	9 −3	10 −4
8.	12 −9	4 −0	15 −8	6 −3	10 −1	18 −9	6 −1	10 −3
9.	13 −6	5 −3	13 −5	2 −0	11 −2	12 −7	9 −6	11 −9
10.	16 −7	8 −6	12 −8	8 −1	16 −9	12 −6	9 −2	14 −5

Subtraction Facts (Form B)

	a	b	c	d	e	f	g	h
1.	10 −7	4 −2	7 −3	15 −6	3 −1	8 −7	10 −5	11 −8
2.	10 −8	8 −3	9 −0	14 −9	6 −4	6 −3	11 −7	16 −7
3.	13 −9	5 −2	9 −5	11 −6	7 −0	8 −5	11 −5	15 −9
4.	12 −6	5 −1	5 −5	13 −4	5 −3	7 −4	15 −8	13 −7
5.	17 −8	9 −7	4 −3	14 −5	9 −2	9 −6	12 −8	10 −6
6.	12 −7	12 −9	8 −4	11 −4	6 −2	9 −3	16 −9	12 −4
7.	14 −6	10 −2	1 −0	16 −8	8 −6	7 −5	15 −7	10 −9
8.	14 −7	10 −4	3 −3	17 −9	7 −1	2 −1	13 −6	13 −5
9.	14 −8	11 −3	7 −2	12 −5	0 −0	6 −5	12 −3	11 −2
10.	18 −9	8 −8	9 −1	13 −8	8 −2	9 −4	11 −9	10 −3

Multiplication Facts (Form A)

	a	b	c	d	e	f	g	h
1.	7 ×2	4 ×8	0 ×4	9 ×1	5 ×3	3 ×3	2 ×7	4 ×1
2.	8 ×6	1 ×5	5 ×2	3 ×2	7 ×0	6 ×6	7 ×9	1 ×3
3.	1 ×7	6 ×5	0 ×6	4 ×7	2 ×6	0 ×2	5 ×4	9 ×0
4.	8 ×7	2 ×8	7 ×8	9 ×2	4 ×2	5 ×5	8 ×5	3 ×9
5.	6 ×4	0 ×0	9 ×3	3 ×4	8 ×4	6 ×7	2 ×5	7 ×6
6.	7 ×3	9 ×4	4 ×6	6 ×3	6 ×8	4 ×9	7 ×7	1 ×1
7.	2 ×9	3 ×5	8 ×3	5 ×0	2 ×1	4 ×3	9 ×6	7 ×5
8.	9 ×9	4 ×5	6 ×9	0 ×8	9 ×8	6 ×2	8 ×2	2 ×4
9.	3 ×6	2 ×2	5 ×7	8 ×8	8 ×1	9 ×5	3 ×8	6 ×1
10.	5 ×8	7 ×4	4 ×4	3 ×7	2 ×3	9 ×7	5 ×9	8 ×9

Multiplication Facts (Form B)

	a	*b*	*c*	*d*	*e*	*f*	*g*	*h*
1.	6 ×2	2 ×2	4 ×5	7 ×8	5 ×7	8 ×8	3 ×2	2 ×0
2.	9 ×2	5 ×6	3 ×3	6 ×3	1 ×9	4 ×4	7 ×7	1 ×4
3.	4 ×6	8 ×9	0 ×9	2 ×3	7 ×6	3 ×1	5 ×8	9 ×6
4.	1 ×0	3 ×4	7 ×5	6 ×4	5 ×5	8 ×7	6 ×5	4 ×3
5.	7 ×9	4 ×7	2 ×9	1 ×2	9 ×5	2 ×4	7 ×4	6 ×0
6.	3 ×5	8 ×6	4 ×8	7 ×3	5 ×4	4 ×2	0 ×7	9 ×7
7.	7 ×2	1 ×6	9 ×4	3 ×6	8 ×0	4 ×9	8 ×5	2 ×5
8.	2 ×8	5 ×3	5 ×9	4 ×0	9 ×8	2 ×6	3 ×7	1 ×8
9.	6 ×8	8 ×2	6 ×7	9 ×9	3 ×8	8 ×4	6 ×6	5 ×1
10.	3 ×9	9 ×3	0 ×5	2 ×7	5 ×2	7 ×1	8 ×3	6 ×9

Division Facts (Form A)

	a	b	c	d	e	f	g
1.	4)16	1)6	8)16	2)10	3)18	4)36	4)4
2.	1)1	6)54	1)7	5)45	9)36	5)35	9)27
3.	8)8	4)12	3)15	7)0	8)24	2)12	4)20
4.	2)8	5)40	9)45	6)48	9)18	5)30	3)0
5.	3)27	1)8	7)63	1)5	4)0	7)14	8)32
6.	9)54	4)32	9)9	6)0	2)14	6)42	8)40
7.	7)28	2)6	5)25	7)21	7)56	2)2	5)5
8.	9)0	4)8	9)63	6)36	8)48	6)12	1)0
9.	5)20	3)3	7)35	2)16	4)28	3)12	7)49
10.	2)4	6)30	8)72	3)21	9)72	6)18	8)56
11.	4)24	1)4	5)15	1)2	7)42	1)3	3)9
12.	1)9	3)24	2)18	6)24	8)64	5)10	9)81

Division Facts (Form B)

	a	b	c	d	e	f	g
1.	3)6̄	5)3̄ 5	7)2̄ 1	1)5̄	8)0̄	2)6̄	8)7̄ 2
2.	6)2̄ 4	8)8̄	3)9̄	9)5̄ 4	5)3̄ 0	1)4̄	6)4̄ 2
3.	5)4̄ 0	7)6̄ 3	6)3̄ 6	2)8̄	4)2̄ 0	8)6̄ 4	3)3̄
4.	2)1̄ 0	4)2̄ 4	4)4̄	9)0̄	1)6̄	5)4̄ 5	8)1̄ 6
5.	9)4̄ 5	3)2̄ 1	8)5̄ 6	1)7̄	3)1̄ 2	9)6̄ 3	2)2̄
6.	6)3̄ 0	5)2̄ 5	2)0̄	7)5̄ 6	2)4̄	7)1̄ 4	4)1̄ 6
7.	5)0̄	9)3̄ 6	6)1̄ 8	3)2̄ 4	6)0̄	3)1̄ 5	7)4̄ 9
8.	1)2̄	8)2̄ 4	2)1̄ 2	8)4̄ 8	9)7̄ 2	4)1̄ 2	1)3̄
9.	9)2̄ 7	4)2̄ 8	7)4̄ 2	4)8̄	5)1̄ 5	1)8̄	9)9̄
10.	1)1̄	5)2̄ 0	3)2̄ 7	6)4̄ 8	7)2̄ 8	6)1̄ 2	8)4̄ 0
11.	7)3̄ 5	2)1̄ 4	9)8̄ 1	1)9̄	4)3̄ 6	5)1̄ 0	2)1̄ 8
12.	4)3̄ 2	6)6̄	8)3̄ 2	3)1̄ 8	9)1̄ 8	2)1̄ 6	6)5̄ 4

Mixed Facts

Add, subtract, multiply, or divide.   Watch the signs.

	a	*b*	*c*	*d*
1.	59 +67	63 −18	23 ×7	6)3954
2.	503 −89	7)9042	596 +87	40 ×68
3.	20)6330	638 +197	603 ×32	420 −237
4.	5967 +848	322 ×24	4273 −695	70)4970
5.	406 ×132	21)275	673 895 +546	7001 −2741
6.	11654 −8465	7468 +4923	5083 ×64	91)6643

Mixed Facts (continued)

Add, subtract, multiply, or divide.   Watch the signs.

	a	*b*	*c*	*d*
7.	2765 4283 +1065	25623 −20736	261 ×100	74)985
8.	594 ×605	26509 8060 +11695	91000 −27624	82)2550
9.	42)8862	958 ×643	94006 73885 +27642	812600 −74607
10.	413000 −324223	88)35288	6072 ×621	780764 +16433
11.	289455 +860950	592006 −93067	48)29314	2409 ×900

PRE-TEST—Addition and Subtraction

Add or subtract.

	a	b	c	d	e	f
1.	3 5 +3	7 +4 3	4 3 +2 5	6 7 +2 8	7 3 +5 2	5 9 +6 3
2.	4 6 −5	5 7 −9	2 8 −1 3	1 4 8 −6 3	1 7 5 −8 6	2 1 4 −3 5
3.	4 2 1 +3 4 8	3 2 5 +4 3 6	7 8 3 +1 9 2	7 5 2 +6 3 8	4 2 8 +1 7 3	9 7 6 +5 4 4
4.	7 3 8 −1 2 5	8 7 2 −4 3 9	9 8 6 −3 9 4	1 4 6 5 −9 3 8	1 8 3 1 −2 5 6	3 8 1 4 −9 1 5

Add or subtract.

	a	b	c	d	c
5.	4 2 1 8 +3 5 7 0	5 8 3 1 +4 1 7 9	6 2 8 1 +3 9 8 2	7 5 4 3 +9 6 4 7	2 7 9 6 +8 2 1 5
6.	7 8 3 2 −4 7 0 1	4 2 1 6 −2 4 3 7	5 2 6 1 4 −8 3 1 6	3 8 1 2 6 −9 4 3 3	4 2 7 1 3 −5 8 1 6
7.	5 3 2 4 6 +3 2 5 1 2	4 2 1 8 6 +1 7 2 8 7	3 8 7 4 3 +4 5 3 8 2	2 0 9 1 7 +3 4 2 1 6	5 2 8 4 3 +2 8 3 7 9
8.	8 2 1 6 5 −3 1 0 4 2	3 2 1 8 6 −9 1 7 8	4 2 5 1 4 −3 4 9 5	8 8 6 7 2 −3 2 9 6 7	9 8 1 3 5 −2 8 4 5 9
9.	4 2 2 6 +3 8	5 2 3 4 1 6 +7 5 8	4 2 8 1 3 8 2 6 +1 4 3 5	4 2 1 6 3 5 2 8 6 +2 5 4 8 8	3 2 8 1 5 1 2 9 1 6 +3 8 4 4 2

A

| | | 4 | 3 | 5 | |

B

| | | 2 | 0 | 1 | |

C

| | 1 | 2 | 3 | |

Solve each problem.

1. Odometer readings, such as shown above, tell how many miles a car has been driven. What is the total number of miles cars A and B have been driven?

   Car A has been driven _____ miles.

   Car B has been driven _____ miles.

   Both cars have been driven _____ miles.

2. How many more miles has car A been driven than car C?

   Car A has been driven _____ miles.

   Car C has been driven _____ miles.

   Car A has been driven _____ more miles.

3. What is the total number of miles car A, car B, and car C have been driven?

   They have been driven _____ miles.

1.

2.

3.

Lesson 1 Addition

Add the ones.
Rename 19 as 10 + 9.

Add the tens.

```
   5 7              7          5 7              5 7
     4              4            4                4
  +6 8            +8         +6 8             +6 8
                1 9 or 10 + 9    9            1 2 9
```

Add.

	a	b	c	d	e	f
1.	3 4 +5	6 +2 1	4 8 +5	9 +3 6	5 6 +3	9 +7 8
2.	3 5 +2 4	4 6 +3 2	3 7 +4 1	2 0 +5 8	3 1 +3 8	6 5 +1 3
3.	5 7 +2 4	3 6 +2 7	5 8 +1 9	5 2 +9 4	3 2 +7 1	5 5 +9 3
4.	3 5 +8 9	7 2 +7 9	8 6 +4 5	4 8 +6 3	3 7 +6 5	5 4 +9 8
5.	3 5 3 +2 1	2 7 1 8 +3 5	4 2 3 +7 0	5 2 1 6 +5 9	3 5 2 7 + 6	5 8 3 7 +2 9
6.	3 6 8 4 2 7 +3 9	4 2 5 9 2 6 + 7	2 1 8 5 4 +2 6	8 3 7 5 8 +7 5	3 1 8 0 6 0 + 9	5 4 5 4 5 4 +5 4

Lesson 2 Subtraction

Rename 72 as "6 tens
and 12 ones."
Subtract the ones.

Rename 1 hundred and
6 tens as "16 tens."
Subtract the tens.

$$
\begin{array}{r} 1\,7\,2 \\ -9\,6 \\ \hline \end{array}
\qquad
\begin{array}{r} {}^{6}\!1\,7\,{}^{12}\!\cancel{2} \\ -9\,6 \\ \hline 6 \end{array}
\qquad
\begin{array}{r} {}^{16}\!{}^{6}\!\cancel{1}\,\cancel{7}\,{}^{12}\!\cancel{2} \\ -9\,6 \\ \hline 7\,6 \end{array}
$$

Subtract.

	a	*b*	*c*	*d*	*e*	*f*
1.	5 7 −3	9 8 −4	6 3 −3	7 5 −6	3 8 −9	4 6 −8
2.	6 8 −2 5	7 5 −3 2	9 8 −4 4	3 7 −1 2	4 6 −3 6	5 8 −2 7
3.	5 3 −2 8	8 4 −3 6	6 1 −2 7	3 7 −1 8	2 5 −1 8	4 2 −2 5
4.	1 5 4 −2 7	1 9 3 −3 7	2 9 5 −2 7	1 4 6 −3 9	2 5 3 −2 7	1 0 4 −4 5
5.	1 6 3 −9 3	2 5 3 −6 2	3 5 7 −7 1	1 7 6 −8 3	4 8 3 −9 3	5 1 9 −3 4
6.	1 8 4 −9 7	3 5 2 −6 9	4 6 3 −8 7	1 0 8 −2 9	5 2 0 −8 3	6 4 5 −9 6

Lesson 3 Addition

	Add the ones.	Add the tens.	Add the hundreds. Rename 16 hundreds as "1 thousand and 6 hundreds."	Add the thousands.

```
        2                  2                   1   2                1   2
    3 3 1 6            3 3 1 6             3 3 1 6             3 3 1 6
      6 2 8              6 2 8               6 2 8               6 2 8
  +8 7 3 7          +8 7 3 7            +8 7 3 7            +8 7 3 7
  ─────────         ─────────           ─────────           ─────────
          1                8 1               6 8 1           1 2 6 8 1
```

Add.

	a	b	c	d	e
1.	4 2 3 +1 6 5	5 2 7 +3 1 9	3 8 2 +4 7 6	5 2 8 +7 3 9	5 2 4 +8 9 8
2.	3 1 6 8 +3 2 4 0	3 7 8 2 +4 5 6 1	8 0 9 3 +1 2 7 9	5 8 3 7 +2 8 9 6	6 7 8 9 +4 5 6 7
3.	5 4 3 1 2 +2 4 2 4 1	5 2 1 6 8 +2 9 2 1 0	8 3 2 4 5 +1 3 8 7 6	4 2 1 0 4 +4 9 8 6 3	5 4 3 7 2 +3 6 7 9 8
4.	4 2 3 1 0 4 +7 3 5	1 4 2 3 3 4 1 0 +6 5 7 8	4 2 1 6 3 8 0 7 1 4 2 1 8	4 2 1 1 6 3 8 4 2 5 +1 0 7 3 1	2 2 4 3 0 3 8 6 5 4 +1 2 4 6 5
5.	5 2 3 1 6 4 2 8 4 +3 7 2 1	3 4 2 1 5 6 3 +7 8 2 1 6	1 4 2 3 7 3 8 6 +2 1 4	4 2 3 0 5 3 1 6 +4 2 1 7	5 2 0 3 4 8 3 1 0 +2 4 4
6.	3 4 2 1 5 3 7 8 6 +4 0 3	2 1 7 3 4 1 6 8 5 2 4 6 +3 7 0 0	4 2 1 5 3 8 0 0 2 4 0 7 +3 1 4 2	1 2 4 2 1 3 3 5 6 8 4 5 4 2 3 +1 3 1 5 4	1 2 4 2 1 1 3 6 8 5 1 7 2 5 6 +6 0 3 8 1
7.	4 2 1 3 8 6 3 4 2 5 +3 8 1 6 0	1 7 2 5 4 2 3 1 1 3 8 2 0 +4 2 1	7 5 2 6 3 8 0 6 2 7 7 6 +5 3 8 1	4 2 7 0 3 8 1 9 7 2 4 4 +4 2 3 1 1	7 3 8 5 2 8 6 5 3 7 6 +2 5 4 0 0

Problem Solving

Solve each problem.

1. A trucker drove 528 kilometers on the first trip and 746 kilometers on the next. How many kilometers did the trucker drive altogether?

   _____ kilometers were driven on the first trip.

   _____ kilometers were driven on the next trip.

   _____ kilometers were driven altogether.

2. Xemo Corporation filled 5,281 orders last week and 7,390 orders this week. How many orders were filled in these two weeks?

   _____ orders were filled last week.

   _____ orders were filled this week.

   _____ orders were filled in the two weeks.

3. Xemo Corporation produced 42,165 xemos in January and 34,895 xemos in February. How many xemos were produced in both January and February?

   _____ xemos were produced in January.

   _____ xemos were produced in February.

   _____ xemos were produced in both months.

4. In three weeks Mr. Jenkins carried the following number of passengers on his bus: 4,216; 3,845; and 7,281. What was the total number of passengers carried in the three weeks?

   _____ passengers were carried.

5. The odometer readings on the last three cars that Mrs. Williams sold were 22,163; 48,395; and 23,842. How many miles were recorded on these three cars?

   _____ miles were recorded.

6. Last month three jets were flown the following number of miles: 42,816; 5,421; and 38,652. What was the total number of miles flown?

   _____ miles were flown.

1.
2.
3.
4.
5.
6.

NAME _____

Lesson 4 Subtraction

	Subtract the ones.	Rename. Subtract the tens.	Subtract the hundreds.	Continue to rename and subtract as needed.

$$
\begin{array}{r} 4\,2\,0\,1\,7 \\ -3\,8\,4\,6 \\ \hline 1 \end{array}
\qquad
\begin{array}{r} {}^{9}\\ 4\,2\,0\,{}^{1}{\cancel{1}}^{10}{\cancel{1}}^{11}\,7 \\ -3\,8\,4\,6 \\ \hline 7\,1 \end{array}
\qquad
\begin{array}{r} {}^{9}\\ 4\,2\,0\,{}^{1}{\cancel{1}}^{10}{\cancel{1}}^{11}\,7 \\ -3\,8\,4\,6 \\ \hline 1\,7\,1 \end{array}
\qquad
\begin{array}{r} {}^{11}{}^{9}\\ {}^{3}{\cancel{4}}\,{}^{1}{\cancel{2}}\,0\,{}^{10}{\cancel{1}}^{11}\,7 \\ -3\,8\,4\,6 \\ \hline 3\,8\,1\,7\,1 \end{array}
$$

Subtract.

	a	b	c	d	e
1.	736 −324	546 −329	831 −480	516 −337	703 −299
2.	4216 −314	2468 −539	5468 −573	2345 −456	1306 −457
3.	5246 −2215	3872 −2438	4351 −2263	4020 −1706	7503 −2455
4.	53211 −4298	42683 −3167	54216 −5299	60831 −7081	29540 −5219
5.	42465 −21528	38429 −14953	76543 −37835	82106 −47297	30907 −18608
6.	67230 −41195	42007 −18246	86992 −20997	71549 −10856	90036 −89595

Problem Solving

Solve each problem.

1. It takes 500 points to win a prize. Abby has 385 points now. How many more points does she need to win a prize?

   _____ points are needed to win a prize.

   Abby now has _____ points.

   She needs _____ more points.

1.

2. There are 1,516 students enrolled at Webb School. Of these, 842 are girls. How many are boys?

   _____ students are enrolled.

   _____ of the students are girls.

   _____ of the students are boys.

2.

3. Factory A employs 5,281 people and factory B employs 3,817 people. How many more people does factory A employ than factory B?

   Factory A employs _____ more people.

3.

4. Mr. Wells had 52,816 miles on his car when he traded it. The car he traded for has 4,357 miles on it. How many fewer miles does it have than the older car?

   It has _____ fewer miles.

4.

5. Last year 42,169 orders were shipped from a warehouse. So far this year 5,837 orders have been shipped. How many more orders must be shipped this year in order to match the total for last year?

   _____ more orders must be shipped.

5.

6. The odometer on Jim's car reads 52,116. The odometer on Pat's car reads 38,429. How many more miles are on Jim's car than are on Pat's car?

   _____ more miles are on Jim's car.

6.

Lesson 5   Addition and Subtraction

Add or subtract.

	a	b	c	d	e	f
1.	32 + 6	5 +48	23 +35	47 +26	89 +50	78 +57
2.	58 −3	72 −21	47 −38	159 −93	143 −85	202 −37
3.	523 +364	428 +537	683 +194	385 +276	483 +629	753 +869
4.	783 −502	926 −418	564 −283	1925 −137	2436 −648	1926 −928
5.	5231 +3468	4661 +2179	3157 +6930	2087 +9237	4281 +6759	
6.	8426 −3312	7531 −3452	8426 −2756	13041 −9158	25308 −8499	
7.	63125 +10420	42163 +45387	28135 +47385	61702 +28715	37839 +57893	
8.	72519 −30418	83162 −35087	52083 −41839	98035 −68746	63613 −55895	
9.	23 34 +42	426 709 +358	4216 5384 +2196	22514 43868 +21706	82965 372 +1451	

Problem Solving

Answer each question.

1. In a contest, Cara earned 758 points. Kelley earned 929 points. Bill earned 1,356 points. How many points did the two girls earn?

   Are you to add or subtract? _____

   How many points did the two girls earn? _____

2. In problem 1, how many more points did Bill earn than Kelley?

   Are you to add or subtract? _____
   How many more points did
      Bill earn than Kelley? _____

3. In problem 1, how many points did all three people earn?

   Are you to add or subtract? _____

   How many points did all three earn? _____

4. This month 32,526 people visited the museum. Last month 28,831 people visited the museum. How many more people visited the museum this month than last month?

   Are you to add or subtract? _____
   How many more people visited the
      museum this month than last month? _____

5. In problem 4, how many people visited the museum during the two months?

   Are you to add or subtract? _____
   How many people visited the
      museum during the two months? _____

6. At the beginning of last year 52,116 cars were registered. There were 4,913 new cars registered the first six months and 3,085 the second six months. How many cars were registered at the end of the year?

   Are you to add or subtract? _____

   How many cars were registered
      at the end of the year? _____

1.
2.
3.
4.
5.
6.

CHAPTER 1 TEST

Add or subtract.

	a	b	c	d	e
1.	42 + 9	75 +83	96 +58	147 +129	345 +286
2.	54 − 6	39 −27	158 −79	384 −215	580 −483
3.	4216 −3817	15382 −8293	42165 −38479	52163 −44318	84362 −53977
4.	5421 +8892	5843 +6969	52816 +32558	4235 6815 +42916	38433 12758 +28906

Answer each question.

5. At the end of last year, suppose the odometer reading on your car was 33,384. You drove your car 29,458 kilometers last year. What was the reading at the beginning of last year?

Are you to add or subtract? _____
What was the reading at
   the beginning of last year? _____

5.

6. In problem 5, suppose you expect to drive the car the same number of kilometers this year as you did last year. If you do, what will the reading be at the end of this year?

Are you to add or subtract? _____
What will the reading be
   at the end of this year? _____

6.

7. Suppose the distances you drove in the last three years were 42,516 kilometers, 38,342 kilometers, and 14,208 kilometers.

How many kilometers did
   you drive in three years? _____

7.

PRE-TEST—Multiplication and Division

Multiply.

	a	b	c	d	e
1.	33 ×3	48 ×4	304 ×2	432 ×8	1234 ×2
2.	6789 ×5	133 ×21	456 ×34	1231 ×22	5783 ×45
3.	123 ×321	576 ×435	1302 ×132	4563 ×478	5009 ×837

Divide.

4. 25)225   14)518   27)463   14)4550   95)3610

5. 53)7832   92)12420   58)45530   32)78216   73)52914

Lesson 1 Multiplication

Multiply.

	a	*b*	*c*	*d*	*e*	*f*	*g*	*h*
1.	4 ×0	2 ×0	8 ×0	1 ×0	7 ×1	6 ×1	1 ×1	5 ×1
2.	8 ×2	2 ×2	4 ×2	7 ×2	6 ×2	5 ×2	3 ×2	9 ×2
3.	9 ×3	7 ×3	5 ×3	0 ×3	1 ×3	6 ×3	4 ×3	3 ×3
4.	4 ×4	3 ×4	5 ×4	8 ×4	7 ×4	0 ×4	9 ×4	1 ×4
5.	8 ×5	2 ×5	7 ×5	5 ×5	4 ×5	3 ×5	1 ×5	0 ×5
6.	8 ×6	2 ×6	9 ×6	7 ×6	6 ×6	5 ×6	1 ×6	3 ×6
7.	9 ×7	7 ×7	6 ×7	0 ×7	1 ×7	5 ×7	8 ×7	4 ×7
8.	0 ×8	5 ×8	8 ×8	9 ×8	4 ×8	3 ×8	6 ×8	7 ×8
9.	3 ×9	9 ×9	8 ×9	1 ×9	2 ×9	7 ×9	6 ×9	4 ×9

Lesson 2 Division

Divide.

	a	b	c	d	e	f	g	h
1.	1)2̄	1)3̄	1)5̄	1)4̄	1)6̄	1)9̄	1)8̄	1)1̄
2.	2)1̄8̄	2)1̄2̄	2)1̄4̄	2)1̄6̄	2)8̄	2)1̄0̄	2)4̄	2)2̄
3.	3)0̄	3)1̄5̄	3)9̄	3)1̄2̄	3)2̄4̄	3)1̄8̄	3)3̄	3)2̄1̄
4.	4)2̄0̄	4)8̄	4)4̄	4)1̄2̄	4)3̄2̄	4)2̄4̄	4)3̄6̄	4)1̄6̄
5.	5)3̄0̄	5)4̄5̄	5)0̄	5)1̄0̄	5)2̄5̄	5)1̄5̄	5)4̄0̄	5)5̄
6.	6)3̄0̄	6)2̄4̄	6)4̄2̄	6)6̄	6)1̄2̄	6)3̄6̄	6)5̄4̄	6)4̄8̄
7.	7)0̄	7)2̄1̄	7)1̄4̄	7)5̄6̄	7)4̄9̄	7)6̄3̄	7)3̄5̄	7)2̄8̄
8.	8)1̄6̄	8)0̄	8)5̄6̄	8)7̄2̄	8)4̄8̄	8)3̄2̄	8)2̄4̄	8)4̄0̄
9.	9)4̄5̄	9)2̄7̄	9)3̄6̄	9)6̄3̄	9)9̄	9)8̄1̄	9)0̄	9)5̄4̄

Lesson 3 Multiplication

Multiply 7 ones by 5.

Multiply 1 ten by 5. Add the 3 tens.

Multiply 8 hundreds by 5.

Multiply 9 thousands by 5. Add the 4 thousands.

```
    3                       3
9 8 1 7    7        9 8 1 7    10
  ×5     ×5           ×5     ×5
─────    ───        ─────    ───
    5    35             8 5    50
                              +30
                            ────
                              80
```

```
   4  3                    4  3
9 8 1 7    800      9 8 1 7    9000
  ×5     ×5           ×5     ×5
─────    ───        ─────    ─────
  0 8 5   4000      4 9 0 8 5   45000
                              +4000
                            ──────
                              49000
```

Multiply.

	a	b	c	d	e
1.	3 2 ×3	2 3 ×4	8 2 ×3	7 8 ×8	9 5 ×6
2.	4 2 1 ×2	1 2 3 ×4	2 4 1 ×3	5 0 1 ×5	1 5 9 ×6
3.	7 8 3 ×3	5 3 8 ×8	7 6 2 ×5	9 5 4 ×7	4 7 3 ×9
4.	1 0 3 3 ×2	3 2 1 6 ×3	3 1 7 2 ×3	5 0 1 4 ×2	3 2 5 7 ×3
5.	1 4 7 8 ×6	5 7 3 8 ×7	4 8 2 6 ×9	5 3 8 4 ×6	7 0 8 3 ×5

Problem Solving

Solve each problem.

1. Mrs. Clarke has 24 employees. Each employee makes 5 units each day. How may units do all employees complete in one day?

   There are _____ employees.

   Each employee makes _____ units each day.

   The employees make _____ units each day.

2. Each bus can carry 77 passengers. How many passengers can be carried on 7 such buses?

   Each bus can carry _____ passengers.

   There are _____ buses in all.

   A total of _____ passengers can be carried.

3. There are 365 days in a year, except leap year which has 366 days. How many days are there in 3 years if there is no leap year included?

   There are _____ days in a year.

   The number of days in _____ years is to be found.

   There are _____ days in 3 years.

4. Seven hundred seventy-five meals were prepared each day for 5 days. How many meals were prepared in the 5 days?

   _____ meals were prepared in the 5 days.

5. Michael earned 3,401 points. His sister earned twice as many. How many points did his sister earn?

   His sister earned _____ points.

6. A machine is designed to produce 2,965 parts each day. How many parts should the machine produce in 7 days?

   The machine should produce _____ parts in 7 days.

1.
2.
3.	4.
5.	6.

Lesson 4 Multiplication

Multiply 4567
by 1.

**Multiply 4567
by 20.**

Multiply 4567
by 300.

```
   4567          4567          4567          4567
  ×321          ×321          ×321          ×321
  ─────         ─────         ─────         ─────
   4567          4567          4567          4567 ⎫
                91340         91340         91340 ⎬ Add.
                             1370100       1370100 ⎭
                                          ─────────
                                          1,466,007
```

Multiply.

1.

```
    5 7          4 8          7 5         1 3 5        2 7 6
   ×2 1         ×3 2         ×6 3         ×4 8         ×4 2
```

2.

```
   5 3 1        8 3 5       1 8 6 4      3 1 8 6      7 0 8 3
    ×2 7         ×9 2         ×2 7         ×5 4         ×9 2
```

3.

```
    4 1 3          5 6 4          2 1 7          9 0 8
   ×2 1 4         ×5 3 2         ×4 1 6         ×5 9 2
```

4.

```
   1 5 6 4        3 8 2 7        9 2 1 6        5 0 4 3
    ×7 9 5         ×6 3 0         ×2 0 5         ×6 8 4
```

Problem Solving

Solve each problem.

1. Each box weighs 28 kilograms. What is the weight of 35 such boxes?

   Each box weighs _____ kilograms.

   There are _____ boxes in all.

   The total weight is _____ kilograms.

2. There are 19 carpenters working for a construction firm. Each worked 47 hours last week. What is the total number of hours they worked last week?

   Each carpenter worked _____ hours.

   There are _____ carpenters in all.

   _____ hours were worked.

3. The production schedule estimates that 321 machines can be produced each week. At that rate, how many machines can be produced in 52 weeks?

   There are _____ machines scheduled to be produced each week.

   There are _____ weeks.

   _____ machines can be produced in 52 weeks.

4. The rail distance between Los Angeles and New York is 3,257 miles. How many miles would a train travel if it made 32 one-way trips between these two cities?

   The train would travel _____ miles.

5. There are 731 cases of zoopers in the warehouse. Each case contains 144 zoopers. How many zoopers are in the warehouse?

   There are _____ zoopers in the warehouse.

6. There are 1,440 minutes in one day. How many minutes are in 365 days?

   There are _____ minutes in 365 days.

1.
2.
3.
4.
5.
6.

Lesson 5 Division

Study how to divide 2074 by 6.

×	100	200	300	400
6	600	1200	1800	2400

2074 is between 1800 and 2400, so 2074 ÷ 6 is between 300 and 400. The hundreds digit is 3.

```
       3
6) 2074
   1800    (300 × 6)
   ────
    274    Subtract.
```

×	10	20	30	40	50
6	60	120	180	240	300

274 is between 240 and 300, so 274 ÷ 6 is between 40 and 50. The tens digit is 4.

```
      34
6) 2074
   1800
   ────
    274
    240    (40 × 6)
    ───
     34    Subtract.
```

×	1	2	3	4	5	6	7
6	6	12	18	24	30	36	42

34 is between 30 and 36, so 34 ÷ 6 is between 5 and 6. The ones digit is 5.

```
                345 r4
           6) 2074
              1800
              ────
               274
               240
               ───
                34
                30    (5 × 6)
   remainder (r)  4   Subtract.
```

Divide.

	a	b	c	d	e
1.	4)92	3)58	3)72	4)77	6)810
2.	3)225	6)590	6)8080	9)4739	6)4254

Problem Solving

Solve each problem.

1. There are 5 people at each table. Two people are standing. There are 92 people in the room. How many tables are there?

There are _____ people in the room.

There are _____ people at each table.

There are _____ tables in the room.

2. Three people earned 774 points in a contest. Suppose each person earned the same number of points. How many points did each person earn?

Each person earned _____ points.

3. As each new car comes off an assembly line, it receives 8 gallons of gasoline. How many new cars can receive gasoline from a tank containing 2,440 gallons?

_____ new cars can receive gasoline.

4. Four baseballs are put in each box. How many boxes are needed to package 273 baseballs? How many baseballs would be left?

_____ boxes are needed.

_____ baseball would be left.

5. A train travels 6,516 miles to make a round-trip between New York and Los Angeles. How many miles would the train travel from Los Angeles to New York?

The train would travel _____ miles.

6. Each carton holds 8 bottles. How many full cartons could be filled with 3,075 bottles? How many bottles would be left over?

_____ cartons could be filled.

_____ bottles would be left over.

1.	
2.	
3.	
4.	
5.	
6.	

Lesson 6   Division

Study how to divide 28888 by 95.

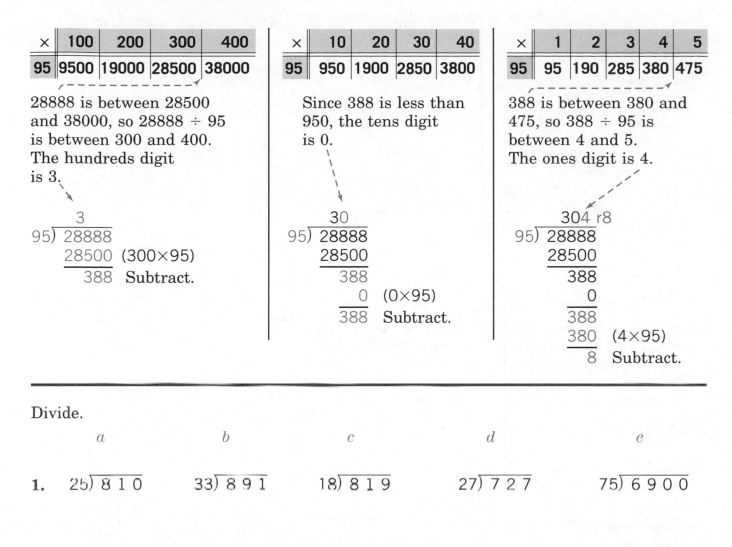

×	100	200	300	400
95	9500	19000	28500	38000

28888 is between 28500 and 38000, so 28888 ÷ 95 is between 300 and 400. The hundreds digit is 3.

```
        3
95) 28888
    28500   (300×95)
      388   Subtract.
```

×	10	20	30	40
95	950	1900	2850	3800

Since 388 is less than 950, the tens digit is 0.

```
       30
95) 28888
    28500
      388
        0   (0×95)
      388   Subtract.
```

×	1	2	3	4	5
95	95	190	285	380	475

388 is between 380 and 475, so 388 ÷ 95 is between 4 and 5. The ones digit is 4.

```
      304 r8
95) 28888
    28500
      388
        0
      388
      380   (4×95)
        8   Subtract.
```

Divide.

	a	b	c	d	e
1.	25) 8 1 0	33) 8 9 1	18) 8 1 9	27) 7 2 7	75) 6 9 0 0
2.	54) 7 6 9 5	28) 9 6 9 8	98) 3 4 9 3 7	75) 3 9 4 0 0	42) 1 4 7 4 2

Problem Solving

Solve each problem.

1. There are 988 units to be shipped. Each crate will hold 26 units. How many crates will be needed to ship all the units?

   There are _____ units to be shipped.

   Each crate will hold _____ units.

   _____ crates will be needed.

2. Mr. Lodey has 987 parts to pack. He will pack 24 parts in each box. How many boxes will he need? How many parts will be left over?

   He will need _____ boxes.

   He will have _____ parts left over.

3. A bank considers 30 days to be a month. How many months would there be in 9,295 days? How many days would be left over?

   There would be _____ months.

   There would be _____ days left over.

4. During a two-week period, 75 employees worked a total of 5,625 hours. Each employee worked the same number of hours. How many hours did each employee work?

   Each employee worked _____ hours.

5. There are 76 sections with a total of 17,100 seats in the new stadium. Each section has the same number of seats. How many seats are in each section?

   There are _____ seats in each section.

6. Three dozen grapefruit are packed in a case. How many cases would be needed to pack 27,100 grapefruit? How many grapefruit would be left over?

   _____ cases would be needed.

   _____ grapefruit would be left over.

1.	2.
3.	4.
5.	6.

Lesson 7 Multiplication and Division

Multiply.

	a	*b*	*c*	*d*	*e*
1.	3 5 ×7	3 4 7 ×5	3 8 5 ×8	1 4 3 8 ×9	4 9 0 6 ×6
2.	3 7 ×8 5	4 8 ×5 4	3 5 7 ×9 2	2 8 9 ×3 8	4 3 5 6 ×2 7
3.	1 5 8 ×1 3 2	7 0 6 ×3 1 5	3 4 5 ×2 2 1	7 0 9 ×7 4 3	6 8 9 ×8 3 8

Divide.

4. 22)3 8 6   35)4 5 2   25)9 5 0   12)1 4 6 8   54)8 4 7 8

5. 15)3 0 9 2   75)4 7 2 8   37)1 5 7 2 5   53)2 4 8 1 5   43)4 5 6 8 3

Problem Solving

Answer each question.

1. It takes 75 hours to make one tractor. How many hours would it take to make 650 tractors?

   Are you to multiply or divide? _____
   How many hours would
     it take to make 650 tractors? _____

2. It takes 28 minutes to make one hubcap. How many hubcaps could be made in 196 minutes?

   Are you to multiply or divide? _____
   How many hubcaps could
     be made in 196 minutes? _____

3. There are 168 hours in one week. How many hours are in 260 weeks?

   Are you to multiply or divide? _____
   How many hours are
     in 260 weeks? _____

4. There were 5,790 tickets sold at the game. There are 75 tickets on a roll of tickets. How many complete rolls of tickets were sold? How many tickets from the next roll were sold?

   Are you to multiply or divide? _____
   How many complete
     rolls of tickets were sold? _____
   How many tickets from the
     next roll were sold? _____

5. A satellite orbits the moon every 45 minutes. How many complete orbits could it make in 5,545 minutes? How many minutes would be left over?

   Are you to multiply or divide? _____
   How many complete
     orbits could be made? _____
   How many minutes
     would be left over? _____

6. There are 10,080 minutes in a week. How many minutes are in 52 weeks?

   Are you to multiply or divide? _____
   How many minutes
     are in 52 weeks? _____

1.	2.
3.	4.
5.	6.

CHAPTER 2 TEST

Multiply.

	a	*b*	*c*	*d*	*e*
1.	4 3 ×2	3 8 ×9	5 0 7 ×8	1 3 5 1 ×6	7 2 5 4 ×7
2.	3 5 ×2 3	4 8 ×7 6	1 5 5 ×3 3	2 0 5 6 ×4 2	3 7 1 8 ×3 7
3.	3 0 4 ×1 4 4	2 1 5 ×2 5 5	1 4 0 3 ×3 0 4	5 5 5 5 ×2 4 6	3 1 8 2 ×3 5 4

Divide.

4. 34) 1 3 6   12) 4 2 0   53) 7 8 1   37) 4 3 1 6   29) 1 7 0 2

5. 74) 9 9 9 0   46) 1 2 5 7   38) 3 8 6 4 0   14) 5 3 8 2 1   63) 2 7 3 4 2

PRE-TEST—Multiplication

Write each answer in simplest form.

	a	*b*	*c*	*d*
1.	$\frac{1}{2} \times \frac{3}{5}$	$\frac{4}{7} \times \frac{4}{5}$	$\frac{2}{3} \times \frac{5}{7}$	$\frac{2}{5} \times \frac{2}{5}$
2.	$\frac{3}{5} \times \frac{1}{6}$	$\frac{3}{8} \times \frac{5}{9}$	$\frac{6}{7} \times \frac{3}{8}$	$\frac{8}{9} \times \frac{3}{10}$
3.	$3 \times \frac{2}{5}$	$5 \times \frac{8}{9}$	$6 \times \frac{3}{4}$	$\frac{8}{9} \times 3$
4.	$4 \times 3\frac{1}{3}$	$2\frac{1}{2} \times 5$	$4 \times \frac{1}{6}$	$\frac{7}{8} \times 12$
5.	$2\frac{1}{3} \times 1\frac{1}{4}$	$1\frac{7}{8} \times 1\frac{2}{7}$	$4\frac{2}{3} \times 1\frac{3}{7}$	$3\frac{1}{3} \times 2\frac{2}{5}$

Lesson 1 Fractions

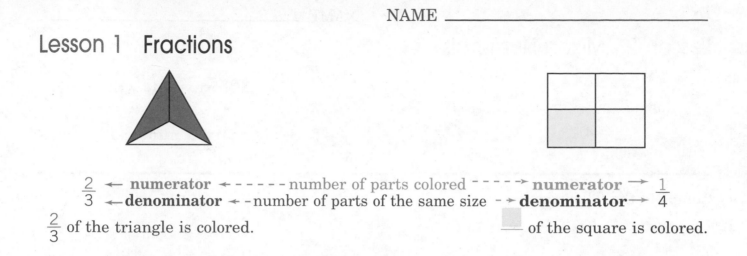

$\frac{2}{3}$ ← **numerator** ← - - - - - number of parts colored - - - - → **numerator** → $\frac{1}{4}$

$\frac{2}{3}$ ← **denominator** ← - number of parts of the same size - → **denominator** → $\frac{1}{4}$

$\frac{2}{3}$ of the triangle is colored.   ▢ of the square is colored.

Write the fraction that tells how much of each figure is colored.

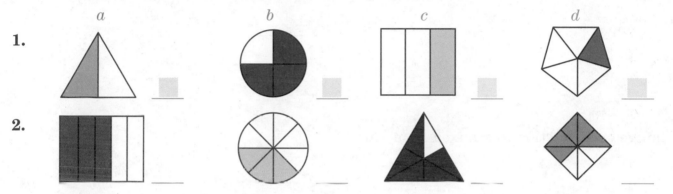

	a	*b*	*c*	*d*
1.				
2.				

Draw a line segment between each fraction and number word that names the same number.

	a			*b*	
3.	one-half	$\frac{4}{5}$		three-eighths	$\frac{7}{9}$
4.	two-thirds	$\frac{3}{4}$		four-sevenths	$\frac{3}{8}$
5.	three-fourths	$\frac{2}{3}$		three-sevenths	$\frac{3}{7}$
6.	four-fifths	$\frac{1}{2}$		seven-eighths	$\frac{4}{7}$
7.	five-sixths	$\frac{5}{6}$		seven-ninths	$\frac{7}{8}$

Write a fraction for each of the following.

	a		*b*	
8.	numerator 4, denominator 7 ____		three-fifths ____
9.	numerator 5, denominator 8 ____		two-sevenths ____
10.	denominator 10, numerator 9 ____		four-ninths ____

Lesson 2   Mixed Numerals

$\frac{13}{4}$ means $\Big\langle$
$13 \div 4$
or
$4\overline{)13}$

$4\overline{)13}$ with $3\frac{1}{4}$ on top

$\frac{12}{1} \to 1 \div 4 = \frac{1}{4}$

$3\frac{1}{4}$ is a short way to write $3 + \frac{1}{4}$.

$3\frac{1}{4}$ is a **mixed numeral**.

Complete the following.

	a	b	c	d
1.	$3\frac{1}{5} = 3 + \underline{\quad}$	$4\frac{1}{2} = \underline{\quad} + \frac{1}{2}$	$3\frac{3}{4} = \underline{\quad} + \underline{\quad}$	$9 + \frac{1}{3} = \underline{\quad}$
2.	$4\frac{2}{3} = 4 + \underline{\quad}$	$5\frac{3}{7} = \underline{\quad} + \frac{3}{7}$	$6\frac{2}{5} = \underline{\quad} + \underline{\quad}$	$8 + \frac{7}{8} = \underline{\quad}$
3.	$5\frac{1}{8} = 5 + \underline{\quad}$	$2\frac{1}{6} = \underline{\quad} + \frac{1}{6}$	$3\frac{1}{3} = \underline{\quad} + \underline{\quad}$	$5 + \frac{3}{7} = \underline{\quad}$

Change each fraction to a mixed numeral.

	a	b	c
4.	$\frac{5}{2}$	$\frac{9}{5}$	$\frac{7}{2}$
5.	$\frac{9}{4}$	$\frac{6}{5}$	$\frac{8}{3}$
6.	$\frac{14}{3}$	$\frac{10}{3}$	$\frac{17}{5}$

Tell whether each of the following is *less than 1*, *equal to 1*, or *greater than 1*.

	a	b	c
7.	$\frac{7}{8}$ _____	$\frac{5}{4}$ _____	$\frac{6}{6}$ _____
8.	$\frac{2}{3}$ _____	$\frac{12}{12}$ _____	$\frac{11}{10}$ _____
9.	$\frac{1}{9}$ _____	$\frac{12}{9}$ _____	$\frac{10}{5}$ _____

28

Lesson 3   Addition

$$\frac{2}{5} + \frac{1}{5} = \frac{2+1}{5}$$ Add the numerators.

$$= \frac{3}{5}$$ Use the same denominator.

$$\begin{array}{r} \frac{2}{5} \\ + \frac{1}{5} \\ \hline \frac{3}{5} \end{array}$$

$$\frac{3}{10} + \frac{4}{10} + \frac{2}{10} = \frac{ + + }{10}$$

$$= \frac{}{10}$$

$$\begin{array}{r} \frac{3}{10} \\ \frac{4}{10} \\ + \frac{2}{10} \\ \hline \end{array}$$

Add.

	a	b	c	d
1.	$\frac{3}{5} + \frac{1}{5} =$	$\frac{4}{8} + \frac{3}{8} =$	$\frac{2}{7} + \frac{2}{7} =$	$\frac{1}{5} + \frac{2}{5} + \frac{1}{5} =$
2.	$\frac{3}{6} + \frac{2}{6} =$	$\frac{1}{7} + \frac{3}{7} =$	$\frac{2}{8} + \frac{1}{8} =$	$\frac{1}{4} + \frac{1}{4} + \frac{1}{4} =$
3.	$\frac{3}{10} + \frac{4}{10} =$	$\frac{4}{12} + \frac{1}{12} =$	$\frac{5}{11} + \frac{4}{11} =$	$\frac{2}{15} + \frac{2}{15} + \frac{7}{15} =$

	a	b	c	d	e	f
4.	$\begin{array}{r}\frac{4}{6}\\+\frac{1}{6}\\\hline\end{array}$	$\begin{array}{r}\frac{3}{8}\\+\frac{4}{8}\\\hline\end{array}$	$\begin{array}{r}\frac{1}{7}\\+\frac{2}{7}\\\hline\end{array}$	$\begin{array}{r}\frac{3}{10}\\+\frac{6}{10}\\\hline\end{array}$	$\begin{array}{r}\frac{7}{12}\\+\frac{4}{12}\\\hline\end{array}$	$\begin{array}{r}\frac{3}{11}\\+\frac{1}{11}\\\hline\end{array}$
5.	$\begin{array}{r}\frac{1}{5}\\\frac{1}{5}\\+\frac{1}{5}\\\hline\end{array}$	$\begin{array}{r}\frac{2}{7}\\\frac{3}{7}\\+\frac{1}{7}\\\hline\end{array}$	$\begin{array}{r}\frac{2}{8}\\\frac{1}{8}\\+\frac{2}{8}\\\hline\end{array}$	$\begin{array}{r}\frac{4}{10}\\\frac{1}{10}\\+\frac{2}{10}\\\hline\end{array}$	$\begin{array}{r}\frac{3}{15}\\\frac{4}{15}\\+\frac{4}{15}\\\hline\end{array}$	$\begin{array}{r}\frac{1}{12}\\\frac{4}{12}\\+\frac{2}{12}\\\hline\end{array}$

Lesson 4 Mixed Numerals to Fractions

$$4\frac{2}{3} = \frac{(3 \times 4) + 2}{3}$$

Multiply the denominator by the whole number and add the numerator.

$$3\frac{1}{6} = \frac{(\ \times\ ) +}{6}$$

$$= \frac{12 + 2}{3}$$

Use the same denominator.

$$= \frac{+}{6}$$

$$= \frac{14}{3}$$

$$= \frac{}{6}$$

Change each mixed numeral to a fraction.

	a	*b*	*c*
1.	$2\frac{5}{8}$	$2\frac{3}{5}$	$3\frac{2}{3}$
2.	$3\frac{7}{10}$	$10\frac{2}{3}$	$14\frac{1}{2}$
3.	$6\frac{7}{8}$	$5\frac{9}{10}$	$13\frac{5}{12}$
4.	$4\frac{5}{6}$	$7\frac{3}{4}$	$8\frac{11}{12}$

Lesson 5 Multiplication

Multiply the numerators.

$$\frac{2}{3} \times \frac{1}{5} = \frac{2 \times 1}{3 \times 5} = \frac{2}{15}$$

Multiply the denominators.

$$\frac{1}{2} \times \frac{3}{4} = \frac{1 \times 3}{2 \times 4}$$

$$= \frac{}{8}$$

$$\frac{2}{5} \times \frac{1}{3} = \frac{\times}{\times}$$

$$=$$

Multiply.

	a	*b*	*c*	*d*
1.	$\frac{1}{2} \times \frac{1}{3}$	$\frac{3}{4} \times \frac{1}{2}$	$\frac{1}{3} \times \frac{1}{4}$	$\frac{3}{5} \times \frac{1}{2}$
2.	$\frac{3}{5} \times \frac{3}{4}$	$\frac{4}{7} \times \frac{3}{5}$	$\frac{4}{5} \times \frac{2}{3}$	$\frac{3}{8} \times \frac{5}{7}$
3.	$\frac{2}{3} \times \frac{4}{5}$	$\frac{1}{8} \times \frac{1}{2}$	$\frac{5}{7} \times \frac{3}{4}$	$\frac{3}{5} \times \frac{7}{8}$
4.	$\frac{6}{7} \times \frac{3}{5}$	$\frac{2}{9} \times \frac{1}{3}$	$\frac{5}{8} \times \frac{3}{7}$	$\frac{2}{7} \times \frac{3}{5}$
5.	$\frac{7}{8} \times \frac{7}{8}$	$\frac{2}{3} \times \frac{2}{3}$	$\frac{4}{9} \times \frac{2}{3}$	$\frac{4}{5} \times \frac{6}{7}$
6.	$\frac{8}{9} \times \frac{5}{7}$	$\frac{5}{8} \times \frac{1}{3}$	$\frac{5}{6} \times \frac{5}{7}$	$\frac{3}{8} \times \frac{5}{8}$

Lesson 6   Renaming Numbers

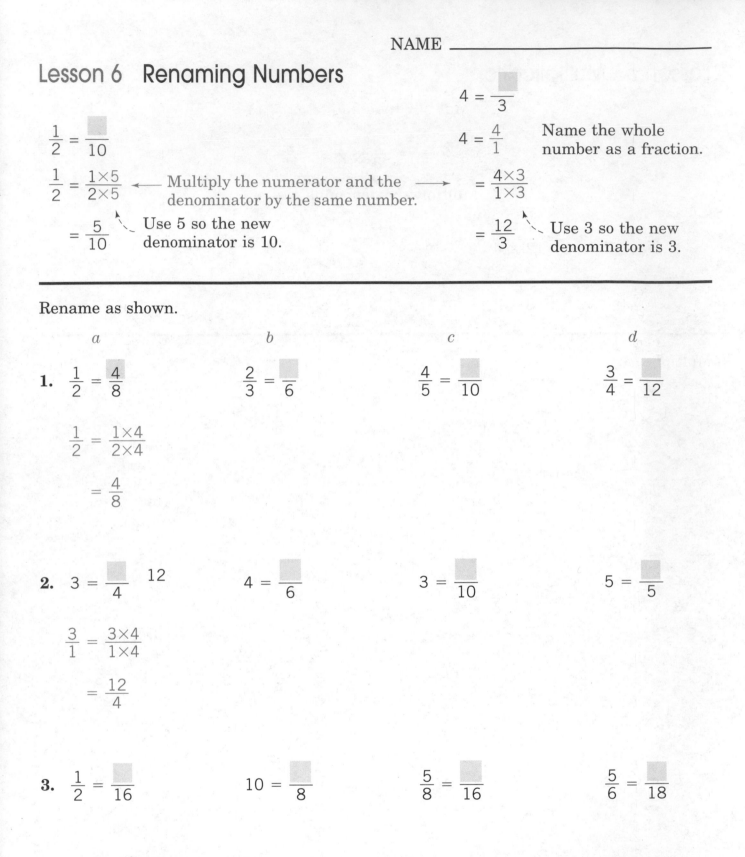

$\dfrac{1}{2} = \dfrac{\blacksquare}{10}$

$\dfrac{1}{2} = \dfrac{1 \times 5}{2 \times 5}$ ⟵ Multiply the numerator and the denominator by the same number. ⟶

$= \dfrac{5}{10}$ Use 5 so the new denominator is 10.

$4 = \dfrac{\blacksquare}{3}$

$4 = \dfrac{4}{1}$ Name the whole number as a fraction.

$= \dfrac{4 \times 3}{1 \times 3}$

$= \dfrac{12}{3}$ Use 3 so the new denominator is 3.

Rename as shown.

       a   *b*   *c*   *d*

1. $\dfrac{1}{2} = \dfrac{4}{8}$ $\dfrac{2}{3} = \dfrac{\blacksquare}{6}$ $\dfrac{4}{5} = \dfrac{\blacksquare}{10}$ $\dfrac{3}{4} = \dfrac{\blacksquare}{12}$

$\dfrac{1}{2} = \dfrac{1 \times 4}{2 \times 4}$

$= \dfrac{4}{8}$

2. $3 = \dfrac{\blacksquare}{4}$ 12 $4 = \dfrac{\blacksquare}{6}$ $3 = \dfrac{\blacksquare}{10}$ $5 = \dfrac{\blacksquare}{5}$

$\dfrac{3}{1} = \dfrac{3 \times 4}{1 \times 4}$

$= \dfrac{12}{4}$

3. $\dfrac{1}{2} = \dfrac{\blacksquare}{16}$ $10 = \dfrac{\blacksquare}{8}$ $\dfrac{5}{8} = \dfrac{\blacksquare}{16}$ $\dfrac{5}{6} = \dfrac{\blacksquare}{18}$

Lesson 7 Greatest Common Factor

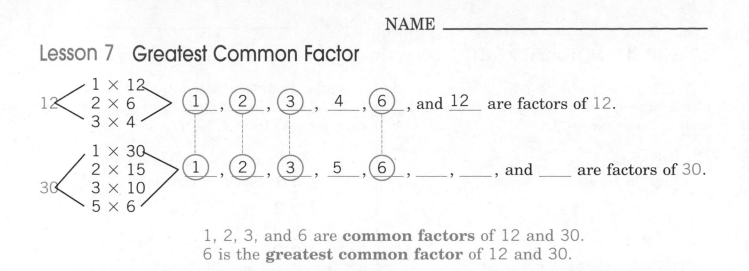

$1, 2, 3,$ ④ , ⑤ , ⑥ are **common factors** of 12 and 30.

6 is the **greatest common factor** of 12 and 30.

List the factors of each number named below. Then list the common factors and the greatest common factor of each pair of numbers.

	factors	common factor(s)	greatest common factor
1. 6	_____		
10	_____	_____	_____
2. 5	_____		
8	_____	_____	_____
3. 12	_____		
15	_____	_____	_____
4. 10	_____		
20	_____	_____	_____
5. 14	_____		
16	_____	_____	_____
6. 15	_____		
7	_____	_____	_____
7. 24	_____		
18	_____	_____	_____

Lesson 8 Simplest Form

A fraction is in simplest form when its numerator and denominator have no common factors, except 1.

Divide 12 and 15 by their greatest common factor.

$$\frac{12}{15} = \frac{12 \div 3}{15 \div 3} = \frac{4}{5}$$

The simplest form for $\frac{12}{15}$ is ___$\frac{4}{5}$___.

A mixed numeral is in simplest form when its fraction is in simplest form and names a number less than 1.

Divide 4 and 6 by their greatest common factor.

$$3\frac{4}{6} = 3 + \frac{4 \div 2}{6 \div 2}$$
$$= 3 + \frac{2}{3}$$
$$= 3\frac{2}{3}$$

The simplest form for $3\frac{4}{6}$ is _____.

Change each of the following to simplest form.

	a	b	c
1.	$\frac{8}{10}$	$\frac{10}{20}$	$\frac{14}{21}$
2.	$2\frac{4}{8}$	$3\frac{6}{9}$	$5\frac{8}{10}$
3.	$\frac{12}{18}$	$5\frac{9}{12}$	$\frac{15}{18}$
4.	$6\frac{8}{12}$	$\frac{25}{30}$	$3\frac{12}{16}$
5.	$\frac{24}{30}$	$3\frac{14}{18}$	$\frac{16}{32}$

Lesson 9 Multiplication

$$\frac{1}{2} \times \frac{3}{4} = \frac{1 \times 3}{2 \times 4}$$
$$= \frac{3}{8}$$

Is $\frac{3}{8}$ in simplest form? _____

$$\frac{4}{5} \times \frac{1}{6} = \frac{4 \times 1}{5 \times 6}$$
$$= \frac{4}{30} \dashrightarrow \frac{4}{30} = \frac{4 + 2}{30 + 2}$$
$$= \frac{2}{15} \dashleftarrow = \frac{2}{15}$$

Is $\frac{4}{30}$ in simplest form? _____
Is $\frac{2}{15}$ in simplest form? _____

Write each answer in simplest form.

	a	b	c	d
1.	$\frac{1}{2} \times \frac{3}{5}$	$\frac{2}{3} \times \frac{4}{5}$	$\frac{2}{3} \times \frac{2}{3}$	$\frac{5}{6} \times \frac{1}{7}$
2.	$\frac{3}{4} \times \frac{4}{5}$	$\frac{5}{6} \times \frac{2}{3}$	$\frac{6}{7} \times \frac{2}{3}$	$\frac{3}{5} \times \frac{4}{9}$
3.	$\frac{5}{6} \times \frac{2}{5}$	$\frac{4}{5} \times \frac{5}{6}$	$\frac{3}{8} \times \frac{2}{3}$	$\frac{2}{10} \times \frac{5}{6}$
4.	$\frac{6}{5} \times \frac{3}{8}$	$\frac{9}{10} \times \frac{5}{12}$	$\frac{8}{9} \times \frac{3}{10}$	$\frac{5}{6} \times \frac{9}{10}$
5.	$\frac{4}{7} \times \frac{5}{6}$	$\frac{3}{8} \times \frac{7}{10}$	$\frac{9}{10} \times \frac{5}{9}$	$\frac{6}{7} \times \frac{9}{10}$

Problem Solving

Solve. Write each answer in simplest form.

1. The Urbans had $\frac{3}{4}$ gallon of milk. One-half of this was used for dinner. How much milk was used for dinner? ($\frac{1}{2}$ of $\frac{3}{4} = \frac{1}{2} \times \frac{3}{4}$)

   1. _____

   _____ gallon was used for dinner.

2. Keara read $\frac{4}{5}$ of a book. Two-thirds of that reading was done at school. How much of the book did she read at school?

   2. _____

   She read _____ of the book at school.

3. Tricia lives $\frac{4}{5}$ mile from work. One morning she ran $\frac{1}{2}$ of the distance to work. How far did Tricia run?

   3. _____

   Tricia ran _____ mile.

4. Three-fourths of a room has been painted. Joseph did $\frac{2}{3}$ of the painting. How much of the room did Joseph paint?

   4. _____

   Joseph painted _____ of the room.

5. A truck was carrying $\frac{3}{4}$ ton of sand. One-third of the sand was put into barrels. How much sand was put into barrels?

   5. _____

   _____ ton of sand was put into barrels.

6. Carrie had a rope that was $\frac{2}{3}$ yard long. She used $\frac{1}{2}$ of it. How much rope did she use?

   6. _____

   _____ yard of rope was used.

7. One-fourth of the people in the room have blue eyes. Two-thirds of the blue-eyed people have blond hair. What part of the people in the room have blond hair and blue eyes?

   7. _____

   _____ have blond hair and blue eyes.

NAME _____

Lesson 10 Multiplication

$4 \times \frac{5}{6} = \frac{4}{1} \times \frac{5}{6}$ Rename whole numbers and mixed numerals as fractions. $4\frac{2}{3} \times 5 = \frac{14}{3} \times \frac{5}{1}$

$= \frac{4 \times 5}{1 \times 6}$ Multiply the fractions. $= \frac{14 \times 5}{3 \times 1}$

$= \frac{20}{6}$ $= \frac{70}{3}$

$= 3\frac{1}{3}$ Change to simplest form. $= 23\frac{1}{3}$

Write each answer in simplest form.

	a	b	c	d
1.	$5 \times \frac{2}{3}$	$6 \times \frac{4}{5}$	$\frac{1}{2} \times 9$	$\frac{3}{4} \times 7$
2.	$9 \times \frac{5}{6}$	$\frac{1}{4} \times 6$	$\frac{3}{8} \times 12$	$10 \times \frac{4}{5}$
3.	$2\frac{1}{2} \times 3$	$1\frac{1}{3} \times 5$	$2 \times 3\frac{2}{5}$	$4 \times 4\frac{2}{3}$

Problem Solving

Solve. Write each answer in simplest form.

1. A can of fruit weighs $\frac{3}{4}$ pound. How many pounds would 3 cans of fruit weigh?

  Three cans of fruit would weigh _____ pounds.

2. A plumber expects a job to take 10 hours. The plumber has already worked $\frac{4}{5}$ of that time. How many hours has the plumber worked?

  The plumber has worked _____ hours.

3. Each book is $\frac{7}{8}$ inch thick. How many inches high would a stack of 12 such books be?

  The stack would be _____ inches high.

4. The carpenter stacked 15 sheets of wallboard on top of each other. If each sheet is $\frac{5}{8}$ inch thick, how high is the stack?

  The stack is _____ inches high.

5. Mark practiced the piano for $\frac{3}{4}$ hour on each of 4 days. How many hours did he practice in all?

  Mark practiced _____ hours in all.

6. Each hamburger weighs $\frac{1}{4}$ pound. How much will 6 hamburgers weigh?

  Six hamburgers will weigh _____ pounds.

7. There are 24 people at a meeting. Suppose $\frac{2}{3}$ of the people are women. How many of the people are women? How many are men?

  _____ of the people are women.

  _____ of the people are men.

1.

2.

3.

4.

5.

6.

7.

Lesson 11 Multiplication

$$2\frac{3}{5} \times 1\frac{1}{6} = \frac{13}{5} \times \frac{7}{6} \quad \text{Change the mixed numerals to fractions.}$$

$$= \frac{13 \times 7}{5 \times 6} \quad \text{Multiply the fractions.}$$

$$= \frac{91}{30}$$

$$= 3\frac{1}{30} \quad \text{Change to simplest form.}$$

Write each answer in simplest form.

	a	b	c	d
1.	$4\frac{2}{3} \times 1\frac{2}{5}$	$3\frac{1}{2} \times 1\frac{1}{6}$	$1\frac{2}{3} \times 2\frac{1}{2}$	$2\frac{2}{3} \times 2\frac{2}{3}$
2.	$2\frac{2}{5} \times 2\frac{1}{4}$	$1\frac{7}{10} \times 2\frac{1}{2}$	$5\frac{1}{3} \times 1\frac{1}{5}$	$2\frac{4}{5} \times 1\frac{1}{7}$
3.	$3\frac{3}{4} \times 2\frac{1}{3}$	$3\frac{2}{5} \times 1\frac{7}{8}$	$4\frac{2}{3} \times 1\frac{1}{8}$	$3\frac{3}{4} \times 3\frac{1}{3}$
4.	$5\frac{1}{6} \times 6\frac{3}{8}$	$2\frac{3}{5} \times 2\frac{1}{2}$	$1\frac{1}{4} \times 1\frac{1}{4}$	$3\frac{1}{8} \times 6\frac{2}{3}$

Problem Solving

Solve. Write each answer in simplest form.

1. A full box of soap weighs $2\frac{2}{3}$ pounds. How many pounds would $1\frac{1}{3}$ boxes of soap weigh?

   They would weigh _____ pounds.

2. It takes $1\frac{4}{5}$ hours to process 1 ton of ore. How many hours would it take to process $3\frac{1}{3}$ tons of ore?

   It would take _____ hours.

3. Each box of bolts weighs $3\frac{3}{4}$ pounds. How many pounds would $8\frac{1}{2}$ boxes of bolts weigh?

   They would weigh _____ pounds.

4. The boys can walk $3\frac{1}{2}$ miles in 1 hour. At that rate, how many miles could the boys walk in $1\frac{1}{6}$ hours?

   The boys could walk _____ miles.

5. Each bag of apples weighs $4\frac{1}{2}$ pounds. How much would $3\frac{1}{2}$ bags of apples weigh?

   They would weigh _____ pounds.

6. Riding her bicycle, Terry averages $9\frac{1}{2}$ miles per hour. At that speed, how far could she go in $2\frac{2}{3}$ hours?

   She could go _____ miles.

7. In problem 6, suppose Terry averages $9\frac{3}{4}$ miles per hour. How far could she go in $2\frac{2}{3}$ hours?

   She could go _____ miles.

8. A machine can process $2\frac{1}{2}$ tons in 1 hour. How many tons can the machine process in $2\frac{1}{10}$ hours?

   The machine can process _____ tons in $2\frac{1}{10}$ hours.

9. If the machine in problem 8 broke down after $1\frac{1}{2}$ hours, how many tons would have been processed?

   _____ tons would have been processed.

| 1. |
| 2. |
| 3. |
| 4. |
| 5. |
| 6. |
| 7. |
| 8. |
| 9. |

CHAPTER 3 TEST

Write each answer in simplest form.

	a	b	c	d
1.	$\dfrac{1}{2} \times \dfrac{5}{6}$	$\dfrac{7}{8} \times \dfrac{5}{6}$	$\dfrac{2}{3} \times \dfrac{5}{7}$	$\dfrac{3}{8} \times \dfrac{3}{8}$
2.	$\dfrac{5}{9} \times \dfrac{6}{7}$	$\dfrac{7}{10} \times \dfrac{8}{9}$	$\dfrac{9}{10} \times \dfrac{5}{6}$	$\dfrac{5}{8} \times \dfrac{4}{5}$
3.	$2 \times \dfrac{3}{5}$	$6 \times \dfrac{5}{7}$	$\dfrac{1}{2} \times 8$	$\dfrac{5}{6} \times 8$
4.	$4 \times 3\dfrac{1}{3}$	$\dfrac{4}{5} \times 2$	$10 \times \dfrac{4}{5}$	$\dfrac{3}{8} \times 10$
5.	$3\dfrac{1}{3} \times 1\dfrac{1}{7}$	$1\dfrac{4}{5} \times 3\dfrac{1}{2}$	$2\dfrac{2}{3} \times 1\dfrac{1}{10}$	$2\dfrac{4}{5} \times 4\dfrac{1}{6}$

PRE-TEST—Addition and Subtraction

Write each answer in simplest form.

	a	b	c	d
1.	$\frac{3}{7}$ $+\frac{1}{7}$	$\frac{4}{9}$ $+\frac{2}{9}$	$\frac{7}{8}$ $-\frac{2}{8}$	$\frac{9}{10}$ $-\frac{3}{10}$
2.	$\frac{2}{3}$ $+\frac{1}{2}$	$\frac{4}{6}$ $+\frac{7}{12}$	$\frac{5}{6}$ $-\frac{3}{8}$	$\frac{9}{10}$ $-\frac{5}{8}$
3.	3 $-\frac{2}{5}$	1 $-\frac{7}{8}$	4 $\frac{3}{5}$ $+\frac{5}{6}$	$\frac{1}{2}$ 3 $+\frac{2}{5}$
4.	$2\frac{3}{4}$ $+\frac{1}{2}$	$\frac{7}{10}$ $+3\frac{7}{8}$	$5\frac{4}{9}$ $-\frac{1}{3}$	$2\frac{7}{12}$ $-\frac{5}{6}$
5.	$5\frac{4}{9}$ $-3\frac{1}{6}$	$7\frac{2}{5}$ $-2\frac{9}{10}$	$2\frac{1}{2}$ $4\frac{1}{3}$ $+3\frac{2}{5}$	$4\frac{1}{2}$ $\frac{5}{6}$ $+3\frac{2}{3}$

Lesson 1   Addition and Subtraction

Add the
numerators.

$$\frac{7}{8} + \frac{5}{8} = \frac{7+5}{8} = \frac{12}{8} = 1\frac{1}{2}$$

Use the same
denominator.

$$\frac{7}{8}$$
$$+\frac{5}{8}$$
$$\frac{12}{8} = 1\frac{1}{2}$$

Subtract the
numerators.

$$\frac{5}{6} - \frac{1}{6} = \frac{5-1}{6} = \frac{4}{6} = \frac{2}{3}$$

Use the same
denominator.

$$\frac{5}{6}$$
$$-\frac{1}{6}$$
$$\frac{4}{6} = \frac{2}{3}$$

- - - - Change to simplest form. - - - -

Write each answer in simplest form.

	a	b	c	d	e
1.	$\frac{1}{5}$ $+\frac{2}{5}$	$\frac{4}{7}$ $+\frac{2}{7}$	$\frac{3}{4}$ $+\frac{2}{4}$	$\frac{5}{6}$ $+\frac{4}{6}$	$\frac{7}{8}$ $+\frac{7}{8}$
2.	$\frac{5}{6}$ $-\frac{4}{6}$	$\frac{7}{8}$ $-\frac{3}{8}$	$\frac{5}{7}$ $-\frac{2}{7}$	$\frac{9}{9}$ $-\frac{4}{9}$	$\frac{5}{8}$ $-\frac{1}{8}$
3.	$\frac{3}{10}$ $+\frac{6}{10}$	$\frac{8}{9}$ $+\frac{4}{9}$	$\frac{3}{8}$ $+\frac{3}{8}$	$\frac{5}{12}$ $+\frac{5}{12}$	$\frac{10}{15}$ $+\frac{14}{15}$
4.	$\frac{11}{12}$ $-\frac{3}{12}$	$\frac{7}{8}$ $-\frac{2}{8}$	$\frac{8}{9}$ $-\frac{5}{9}$	$\frac{9}{10}$ $-\frac{4}{10}$	$\frac{9}{16}$ $-\frac{3}{16}$
5.	$\frac{7}{12}$ $+\frac{8}{12}$	$\frac{5}{9}$ $-\frac{2}{9}$	$\frac{8}{15}$ $+\frac{10}{15}$	$\frac{7}{10}$ $-\frac{3}{10}$	$\frac{6}{14}$ $+\frac{6}{14}$

Problem Solving

Solve. Write each answer in simplest form.

1. Preston drank $\frac{1}{4}$ gallon of milk yesterday and $\frac{1}{4}$ gallon of milk today. What part of a gallon of milk did he drink during these two days?

   He drank _____ gallon of milk.

2. Trina and Jamie have painted $\frac{3}{4}$ of a room. Jamie painted $\frac{1}{4}$ of the room. How much of the room did Trina paint?

   Trina painted _____ of the room.

3. Tom measured two boards. He found that each was $\frac{3}{8}$ inch thick. What would be the total thickness of the boards if he glues them together?

   The total thickness would be _____ inch.

4. An unopened box of cereal weighed $\frac{15}{16}$ pound. Mother used $\frac{5}{16}$ pound of cereal from the box. How much cereal remains in the box?

   _____ pound remains in the box.

5. A television show has just begun and will last $\frac{5}{6}$ hour. After $\frac{4}{6}$ hour, what part of an hour remains of the television show?

   _____ hour remains of the television show.

6. Tess jogged $\frac{3}{4}$ hour before work. That same day she jogged $\frac{3}{4}$ hour after work. How long did she jog in all that day?

   She jogged _____ hours that day.

7. Max spent $\frac{5}{6}$ hour typing. He spent $\frac{1}{6}$ hour proofreading his typing. How long did he spend typing and proofreading in all?

   He spent _____ hour typing and proofreading.

8. In problem 7, how much longer did he spend typing than proofreading?

   He spent _____ hour more typing than proofreading.

1.	2.
3.	4.
5.	6.
7.	8.

44

Lesson 2 Addition and Subtraction

$$\frac{2}{3} \begin{array}{c} \times 2 \\ \hline \times 2 \end{array} = \frac{4}{6}$$

$$+\frac{1}{2} \begin{array}{c} \times 3 \\ \hline \times 3 \end{array} = +\frac{3}{6}$$

$$\frac{7}{6} = 1\frac{1}{6}$$

The denominators are 3 and 2. Since $2 \times 3 = 6$, rename each fraction with a denominator of 6.

Add or subtract the fractions.

Write the answer in simplest form.

$$\frac{2}{3} \begin{array}{c} \times 2 \\ \hline \times 2 \end{array} = \frac{4}{6}$$

$$-\frac{1}{2} \begin{array}{c} \times 3 \\ \hline \times 3 \end{array} = -\frac{3}{6}$$

$$\frac{1}{6}$$

Write each answer in simplest form.

	a	b	c	d
1.	$\frac{3}{5}$ $+\frac{2}{3}$	$\frac{5}{6}$ $+\frac{1}{5}$	$\frac{1}{2}$ $+\frac{1}{3}$	$\frac{3}{10}$ $+\frac{1}{3}$
2.	$\frac{2}{3}$ $-\frac{1}{4}$	$\frac{5}{6}$ $-\frac{2}{5}$	$\frac{7}{8}$ $-\frac{2}{3}$	$\frac{3}{4}$ $-\frac{1}{3}$
3.	$\frac{7}{8}$ $+\frac{1}{3}$	$\frac{7}{8}$ $-\frac{1}{3}$	$\frac{2}{5}$ $+\frac{3}{4}$	$\frac{1}{2}$ $-\frac{1}{3}$
4.	$\frac{1}{3}$ $+\frac{3}{4}$	$\frac{3}{5}$ $-\frac{1}{3}$	$\frac{1}{2}$ $+\frac{4}{5}$	$\frac{3}{4}$ $-\frac{2}{3}$

Lesson 3 Addition and Subtraction

$$\frac{3}{4} \times \frac{3}{3} \quad \frac{9}{12}$$
$$+\frac{1}{6} \times \frac{2}{2} \quad +\frac{2}{12}$$
$$\overline{\frac{11}{12}}$$

The denominators are 4 and 6. Since $3 \times 4 = 12$ and $2 \times 6 = 12$, rename each fraction with a denominator of 12.

Add the fractions.

$$\frac{9}{10} \longrightarrow \frac{9}{10}$$
$$-\frac{2}{5} \quad \times 2 \quad -\frac{4}{10}$$
$$\overline{\frac{5}{10}} = \frac{1}{2}$$

The denominators are 5 and 10. Since $2 \times 5 = 10$, rename only $\frac{2}{5}$ with a denominator of 10. Subtract the fractions.

Change to simplest form.

Write each answer in simplest form.

	a	*b*	*c*	*d*
1.	$\frac{2}{5}$ $+\frac{1}{2}$	$\frac{2}{5}$ $+\frac{1}{3}$	$\frac{3}{4}$ $+\frac{1}{2}$	$\frac{7}{8}$ $+\frac{1}{4}$
2.	$\frac{2}{3}$ $-\frac{1}{4}$	$\frac{3}{5}$ $-\frac{1}{2}$	$\frac{2}{3}$ $-\frac{1}{6}$	$\frac{1}{2}$ $-\frac{3}{10}$
3.	$\frac{9}{10}$ $+\frac{1}{2}$	$\frac{5}{6}$ $-\frac{3}{4}$	$\frac{5}{6}$ $+\frac{1}{2}$	$\frac{7}{10}$ $-\frac{1}{5}$
4.	$\frac{2}{3}$ $+\frac{5}{6}$	$\frac{11}{12}$ $-\frac{1}{4}$	$\frac{5}{6}$ $+\frac{3}{10}$	$\frac{9}{10}$ $-\frac{1}{2}$

Lesson 4 Addition

$3\frac{1}{2} \longrightarrow 3\frac{4}{8}$

$+1\frac{1}{8} \longrightarrow +1\frac{1}{8}$

$\phantom{+1\frac{1}{8} \longrightarrow} 4\frac{5}{8}$

Rename the numbers so the fractions have the same denominator.
Add the fractions.
Add the whole numbers.

$1\frac{1}{2} \longrightarrow 1\frac{6}{12}$

$3\frac{3}{4} \longrightarrow 3\frac{9}{12}$

$+\frac{2}{3} \longrightarrow +\frac{8}{12}$

Change to simplest form.

$4\frac{23}{12} = 5\frac{11}{12}$

Write each answer in simplest form.

	a	b	c	d

1.
a: $3\frac{1}{4}$ $+2\frac{4}{5}$

b: $3\frac{1}{6}$ $+\frac{3}{4}$

c: $5\frac{1}{2}$ $+1\frac{5}{8}$

d: $3\frac{11}{12}$ $+\frac{5}{6}$

2.
a: $9\frac{7}{8}$ $+\frac{3}{4}$

b: $7\frac{2}{5}$ $+4\frac{3}{10}$

c: $\frac{3}{5}$ $+2\frac{5}{6}$

d: $\frac{9}{10}$ $+3\frac{5}{6}$

3.
a: $6\frac{2}{3}$ $1\frac{3}{4}$ $+\frac{1}{6}$

b: $2\frac{1}{5}$ $2\frac{1}{4}$ $+1\frac{1}{2}$

c: $3\frac{1}{3}$ $\frac{5}{6}$ $+3\frac{7}{12}$

d: $\frac{1}{2}$ $5\frac{1}{5}$ $+1\frac{3}{10}$

4.
a: $\frac{3}{5}$ $1\frac{2}{3}$ $+2\frac{1}{2}$

b: $3\frac{5}{8}$ $2\frac{1}{6}$ $+\frac{5}{12}$

c: $\frac{1}{4}$ $1\frac{1}{2}$ $+4\frac{7}{8}$

d: $2\frac{2}{3}$ $2\frac{1}{2}$ $+3\frac{2}{5}$

Lesson 5 Subtraction

$3\frac{2}{3} \longrightarrow 3\frac{4}{6}$

$-1\frac{1}{6} \longrightarrow -1\frac{1}{6}$

$\overline{\qquad\qquad\qquad} \quad \overline{2\frac{3}{6} = 2\frac{1}{2}}$

Rename the numbers so the fractions have the same denominator.
Subtract the fractions.
Subtract the whole numbers.

Change to simplest form.

$3 \longrightarrow 2\frac{4}{4}$

$-\frac{1}{4} \longrightarrow -\frac{1}{4}$

$\overline{\qquad\qquad} \quad \overline{2\frac{3}{4}}$

$3 = 2 + 1$
$= 2 + \frac{4}{4}$
$= 2\frac{4}{4}$

Write each answer in simplest form.

	a	*b*	*c*	*d*
1.	7	4	5	8
	$-\frac{3}{4}$	$-\frac{1}{2}$	$-\frac{2}{3}$	$-\frac{1}{8}$
2.	$3\frac{4}{5}$	$5\frac{2}{3}$	$4\frac{5}{6}$	$5\frac{9}{10}$
	$-1\frac{1}{2}$	$-3\frac{4}{9}$	$-1\frac{1}{2}$	$-3\frac{2}{5}$
3.	5	$6\frac{3}{4}$	$2\frac{2}{3}$	10
	$-\frac{3}{5}$	$-5\frac{1}{8}$	$-1\frac{1}{2}$	$-2\frac{3}{10}$
4.	$10\frac{5}{6}$	8	$9\frac{5}{6}$	6
	$-7\frac{5}{12}$	$-\frac{5}{8}$	$-2\frac{1}{3}$	$-\frac{9}{10}$

Lesson 6 Subtraction

Rename the numbers so the fractions
have the same denominator.

Rename $3\frac{3}{12}$ so you can
subtract the fractions.

Rename $4\frac{5}{10}$ so you can
subtract the fractions.

$3\frac{1}{4} \longrightarrow 3\frac{3}{12} \longrightarrow 2\frac{15}{12}$ $\begin{aligned} 3\frac{3}{12} &= 2 + 1\frac{3}{12} \\ &= 2 + \frac{15}{12} \\ &= 2\frac{15}{12} \end{aligned}$ $4\frac{1}{2} \longrightarrow 4\frac{5}{10} \longrightarrow 3\frac{15}{10}$ $\begin{aligned} 4\frac{5}{10} &= 3 + 1\frac{5}{10} \\ &= 3 + \frac{15}{10} \\ &= 3\frac{15}{10} \end{aligned}$

$-1\frac{5}{6} \longrightarrow -1\frac{10}{12} \longrightarrow -1\frac{10}{12}$ $-1\frac{3}{5} \longrightarrow -1\frac{6}{10} \longrightarrow -1\frac{6}{10}$

$1\frac{5}{12}$ $2\frac{9}{10}$

Write each answer in simplest form.

	a	b	c	d

1. $2\frac{1}{2}$ $5\frac{1}{4}$ $7\frac{3}{4}$ $6\frac{2}{5}$

$-1\frac{3}{4}$ $-4\frac{1}{3}$ $-3\frac{5}{6}$ $-4\frac{1}{2}$

2. $8\frac{3}{8}$ $5\frac{1}{4}$ $3\frac{7}{12}$ $4\frac{1}{6}$

$-1\frac{7}{8}$ $-4\frac{3}{4}$ $1\frac{3}{4}$ $-2\frac{3}{8}$

3. $9\frac{1}{2}$ $6\frac{1}{3}$ $11\frac{1}{6}$ $3\frac{3}{10}$

$-5\frac{7}{10}$ $-3\frac{5}{6}$ $-4\frac{5}{12}$ $-2\frac{1}{2}$

4. $7\frac{3}{4}$ $12\frac{1}{4}$ $15\frac{1}{2}$ $10\frac{1}{6}$

$-5\frac{4}{5}$ $-6\frac{5}{8}$ $-8\frac{2}{3}$ $-3\frac{3}{4}$

Problem Solving

Solve. Write each answer in simplest form.

1. A CD has been playing for $\frac{1}{3}$ hour. The CD still has $\frac{5}{12}$ hour to play. What is the total length of time the CD can play?

   The CD can play _____ hour.

2. It rained $\frac{3}{4}$ inch yesterday and $\frac{3}{10}$ inch today. How much more did it rain yesterday?

   It rained _____ inch more yesterday.

3. Matthew spent $\frac{1}{2}$ hour doing his history homework and $\frac{3}{4}$ hour doing his science homework. How much time did he spend doing homework?

   He spent _____ hours doing homework.

4. Rob has a board that is $\frac{1}{8}$ inch too wide. The board is $\frac{3}{4}$ inch wide. What width board does Rob need?

   Rob needs a board _____ inch wide.

5. Maranda read $\frac{3}{5}$ hour in the morning and $\frac{1}{2}$ hour in the afternoon. How many hours did she read in the morning and afternoon?

   She read _____ hours.

6. In problem 5, how much longer did she read in the morning than in the afternoon?

   She read _____ hour longer in the morning.

7. John has two boxes. One weighs $\frac{3}{10}$ pound and the other weighs $\frac{7}{8}$ pound. What is the combined weight of both boxes?

   The combined weight is _____ pounds.

8. In problem 7, how much more does the heavier box weigh?

   The heavier box weighs _____ pound more.

1.
2.
3.
4.
5.
6.
7.
8.

Lesson 7   Addition and Subtraction

Write each answer in simplest form.

	a	*b*	*c*	*d*
1.	$\dfrac{7}{8}$ $+\dfrac{5}{8}$	$\dfrac{9}{16}$ $-\dfrac{3}{16}$	$\dfrac{3}{5}$ $+\dfrac{2}{5}$	$\dfrac{11}{12}$ $-\dfrac{3}{12}$
2.	$\dfrac{1}{2}$ $+\dfrac{7}{8}$	$\dfrac{4}{5}$ $-\dfrac{2}{3}$	$\dfrac{4}{9}$ $+\dfrac{5}{6}$	$\dfrac{3}{4}$ $-\dfrac{5}{12}$
3.	9 $-\dfrac{5}{9}$	1 $-\dfrac{3}{10}$	4 $\dfrac{3}{8}$ $+\dfrac{3}{4}$	$\dfrac{7}{12}$ $\dfrac{2}{3}$ $+7$
4.	$\dfrac{2}{3}$ $+3\dfrac{4}{5}$	$7\dfrac{3}{8}$ $-\dfrac{2}{3}$	$6\dfrac{1}{6}$ $+\dfrac{5}{12}$	$1\dfrac{2}{5}$ $-\dfrac{7}{10}$
5.	$14\dfrac{3}{4}$ $-3\dfrac{11}{12}$	$16\dfrac{11}{12}$ $-2\dfrac{1}{6}$	$3\dfrac{2}{3}$ $2\dfrac{1}{5}$ $+4\dfrac{3}{8}$	$2\dfrac{5}{6}$ $3\dfrac{1}{5}$ $+2\dfrac{3}{10}$

Problem Solving

Today's Workouts	
Kerri	$1\frac{1}{2}$ hours
Jennifer	$\frac{3}{4}$ hour
Ahmad	2 hours
Risa	$\frac{2}{3}$ hour

Solve. Write each answer in simplest form.

1. Who had a longer workout, Jennifer or Risa? How much longer?

   _____ had a longer workout.

   It was _____ hour longer.

2. How much longer was Ahmad's workout than Kerri's workout?

   Ahmad's workout was _____ hour longer.

3. Risa finished her workout just as Kerri started hers. How long did it take from the time Risa started until Kerri finished?

   It took _____ hours.

4. Kerri and Jennifer started their workouts at the same time. When Jennifer finished her workout, how much longer did Kerri have to finish her workout?

   She had _____ hour left to finish her workout.

5. What was the total workout time for all four people on the list?

   The total workout time was _____ hours.

6. What is the difference between the longest workout time and the shortest workout time?

   The difference is _____ hours.

1.

2.

3.

4.

5.

6.

52

CHAPTER 4 TEST

Write each answer in simplest form.

	a	b	c	d

1.

a
$\frac{3}{8}$
$+\frac{4}{8}$

b
$\frac{7}{10}$
$-\frac{2}{10}$

c
$\frac{5}{12}$
$+\frac{9}{12}$

d
$\frac{8}{9}$
$-\frac{6}{9}$

2.

$\frac{5}{6}$
$+\frac{2}{9}$

$\frac{7}{8}$
$+\frac{1}{3}$

$\frac{9}{10}$
$-\frac{2}{5}$

$\frac{3}{4}$
$-\frac{2}{3}$

3.

6
$-\frac{1}{9}$

3
$-\frac{4}{7}$

$\frac{3}{8}$
$\frac{5}{6}$
$+4$

$\frac{7}{8}$
2
$+\frac{3}{4}$

4.

$4\frac{5}{6}$
$+\frac{3}{5}$

$\frac{3}{8}$
$+2\frac{9}{10}$

$6\frac{3}{8}$
$-\frac{5}{6}$

$7\frac{1}{4}$
$-\frac{7}{12}$

5.

$6\frac{3}{5}$
$+2\frac{3}{4}$

$4\frac{5}{8}$
$-1\frac{1}{2}$

$9\frac{1}{8}$
$2\frac{4}{6}$
$+\frac{7}{10}$

$5\frac{3}{4}$
$\frac{1}{6}$
$+5\frac{3}{8}$

PRE-TEST—Division

Write each answer in simplest form.

	a	b	c	d
1.	$4 \div \frac{1}{2}$	$7 \div \frac{2}{3}$	$8 \div \frac{4}{5}$	$9 \div \frac{6}{7}$
2.	$\frac{1}{4} \div 2$	$\frac{3}{5} \div 2$	$\frac{3}{7} \div 3$	$\frac{8}{9} \div 6$
3.	$\frac{1}{7} \div \frac{1}{2}$	$\frac{1}{8} \div \frac{1}{4}$	$\frac{1}{4} \div \frac{1}{8}$	$\frac{1}{6} \div \frac{1}{7}$
4.	$\frac{1}{8} \div \frac{1}{10}$	$\frac{3}{5} \div \frac{2}{3}$	$\frac{4}{7} \div \frac{2}{7}$	$\frac{5}{6} \div \frac{5}{8}$
5.	$7\frac{1}{2} \div 10$	$3 \div 1\frac{1}{5}$	$\frac{1}{4} \div 1\frac{1}{6}$	$2\frac{1}{2} \div 1\frac{1}{6}$

Lesson 1 Reciprocals

The product of any number and its **reciprocal** is 1.

reciprocals

$$\frac{2}{3} \times \frac{3}{2} = \frac{2 \times 3}{3 \times 2} = \frac{6}{6} = 1$$

The reciprocal of $\frac{2}{3}$ is $\underline{\frac{3}{2}}$.

The reciprocal of $\frac{3}{2}$ is _____.

reciprocals

$$\frac{1}{2} \times \frac{2}{1} = \frac{1 \times 2}{2 \times 1} = \frac{2}{2} = 1$$

The reciprocal of $\frac{1}{2}$ is $\underline{\frac{2}{1}}$ or $\underline{2}$.

The reciprocal of 2 is _____.

Write the reciprocal of each of the following.

	a	b	c	d	e	f
1.	$\frac{3}{5}$ ___	$\frac{7}{8}$ ___	$\frac{4}{5}$ ___	$\frac{5}{7}$ ___	$\frac{4}{9}$ ___	$\frac{6}{7}$ ___
2.	$\frac{5}{3}$ ___	$\frac{8}{7}$ ___	$\frac{5}{4}$ ___	$\frac{7}{5}$ ___	$\frac{9}{4}$ ___	$\frac{7}{6}$ ___
3.	$\frac{1}{8}$ ___	$\frac{1}{3}$ ___	$\frac{1}{4}$ ___	$\frac{1}{9}$ ___	$\frac{1}{16}$ ___	$\frac{1}{14}$ ___
4.	$\frac{8}{1}$ ___	$\frac{3}{1}$ ___	$\frac{4}{1}$ ___	$\frac{9}{1}$ ___	$\frac{16}{1}$ ___	$\frac{14}{1}$ ___
5.	8 ___	3 ___	4 ___	9 ___	16 ___	14 ___
6.	$\frac{8}{5}$ ___	6 ___	$\frac{2}{3}$ ___	$\frac{11}{6}$ ___	$\frac{7}{4}$ ___	12 ___
7.	15 ___	$\frac{10}{9}$ ___	$\frac{12}{11}$ ___	17 ___	$\frac{8}{9}$ ___	$\frac{17}{2}$ ___
8.	$\frac{15}{8}$ ___	$\frac{5}{12}$ ___	11 ___	$\frac{7}{11}$ ___	$\frac{1}{11}$ ___	$\frac{17}{3}$ ___
9.	$\frac{10}{1}$ ___	13 ___	$\frac{1}{17}$ ___	$\frac{5}{11}$ ___	$\frac{9}{7}$ ___	5 ___
10.	$\frac{5}{8}$ ___	$\frac{1}{6}$ ___	7 ___	$\frac{12}{7}$ ___	2 ___	$\frac{2}{5}$ ___

Lesson 2   Division

$$15 \div \frac{3}{4} = \frac{15}{1} \times \frac{4}{3}$$

To divide by a fraction, multiply by its reciprocal.

$$10 \div \frac{6}{7} = \frac{10}{1} \times \frac{7}{6}$$

$$= \frac{15 \times 4}{1 \times 3}$$

Multiply the fractions.

$$= \frac{10 \times 7}{1 \times 6}$$

Write the answer in simplest form.

$$= \frac{60}{3}$$

$$= \frac{70}{6}$$

$$= 20$$

$$= 11\frac{2}{3}$$

Write each answer in simplest form.

	a	b	c	d
1.	$10 \div \frac{1}{3}$	$8 \div \frac{1}{2}$	$7 \div \frac{1}{4}$	$6 \div \frac{1}{5}$
2.	$14 \div \frac{2}{7}$	$15 \div \frac{2}{5}$	$16 \div \frac{3}{8}$	$18 \div \frac{5}{9}$
3.	$18 \div \frac{1}{3}$	$14 \div \frac{7}{8}$	$17 \div \frac{1}{2}$	$12 \div \frac{3}{4}$

Lesson 3 Division

$$\frac{1}{2} \div 4 = \frac{1}{2} \times \frac{1}{4}$$

To divide by a whole number, multiply by its reciprocal.

$$= \frac{1 \times 1}{2 \times 4}$$

Multiply the fractions.

$$= \frac{1}{8}$$

To divide $\frac{1}{2}$ by 4,

multiply $\frac{1}{2}$ by _____.

$$\frac{2}{3} \div 5 = \frac{2}{3} \times \frac{1}{5}$$

$$= \frac{2 \times 1}{3 \times 5}$$

$$= \frac{2}{15}$$

To divide $\frac{2}{3}$ by 5,

multiply $\frac{2}{3}$ by _____.

Write each answer in simplest form.

	a	b	c	d
1.	$\frac{1}{2} \div 6$	$\frac{1}{4} \div 2$	$\frac{1}{3} \div 5$	$\frac{1}{6} \div 2$
2.	$\frac{3}{5} \div 4$	$\frac{5}{8} \div 2$	$\frac{3}{4} \div 4$	$\frac{5}{6} \div 3$
3.	$\frac{3}{4} \div 6$	$\frac{2}{3} \div 6$	$\frac{4}{5} \div 4$	$\frac{5}{6} \div 10$

Problem Solving

Solve. Write each answer in simplest form.

1. One-third pound of flour is separated into 2 bowls. The same amount of flour is in each bowl. How much flour is in each bowl?

    _____ pound is in each bowl.

2. One-half of a room is painted. Each of 4 people did the same amount of painting. How much of the room did each person paint?

    Each person painted _____ of the room.

3. Kevin used $\frac{3}{4}$ gallon of gasoline to mow a lawn 3 times. How much gasoline did he use to mow the lawn once?

    He used _____ gallon.

4. A string $\frac{2}{3}$ yard long is cut into 4 pieces. Each piece is the same length. How long is each piece?

    Each piece is _____ yard long.

5. Seven-eighths gallon of liquid is poured into 4 containers. Each container has the same amount in it. How much liquid is in each container?

    _____ gallon is in each container.

6. The students have $\frac{1}{2}$ hour to complete 3 sections of a quiz. They have the same amount of time to do each section. How much time do they have for each section of the quiz?

    They have _____ hour to do each section.

1.
2.
3.
4.
5.
6.

58

Lesson 4 Division

Multiply by
the reciprocal.

$$\frac{1}{4} \div \frac{1}{3} = \frac{1}{4} \times \frac{3}{1}$$

$$= \frac{1 \times 3}{4 \times 1}$$

$$= \frac{3}{4}$$

Multiply by
the reciprocal.

$$\frac{3}{4} \div \frac{1}{2} = \frac{3}{4} \times \frac{2}{1}$$

$$= \frac{3 \times 2}{4 \times 1}$$

$$= \frac{6}{4}$$ Write the
answer in
simplest form.

$$= 1\frac{2}{4}$$

$$= 1\frac{1}{2}$$

Write each answer in simplest form.

	a	b	c	d
1.	$\frac{1}{5} \div \frac{1}{2}$	$\frac{1}{3} \div \frac{1}{2}$	$\frac{1}{8} \div \frac{1}{4}$	$\frac{1}{9} \div \frac{1}{6}$
2.	$\frac{3}{5} \div \frac{1}{2}$	$\frac{4}{7} \div \frac{2}{3}$	$\frac{4}{5} \div \frac{1}{10}$	$\frac{5}{6} \div \frac{2}{3}$
3.	$\frac{4}{5} \div \frac{2}{5}$	$\frac{3}{8} \div \frac{3}{4}$	$\frac{4}{9} \div \frac{1}{5}$	$\frac{7}{8} \div \frac{7}{10}$

Problem Solving

Solve. Write each answer in simplest form.

1. How many $\frac{1}{6}$-hour sessions are there in $\frac{1}{2}$ hour?

   There are _____ sessions.

2. Erika has a ribbon $\frac{3}{4}$ yard long. How many $\frac{1}{4}$-yard pieces can she get from her ribbon?

   She can get _____ pieces.

3. In problem 2, how many $\frac{1}{8}$-yard pieces can Erika get from her ribbon?

   She can get _____ pieces.

4. A machine uses gas at the rate of $\frac{1}{5}$ gallon an hour. So far $\frac{9}{10}$ gallon has been used. How many hours has the machine operated?

   The machine has operated _____ hours.

5. Suppose the machine in problem 4 has used $\frac{4}{5}$ gallon of gas. How many hours did the machine operate?

   The machine operated _____ hours.

6. Three-eighths pound of nuts is put in each bag. How many bags can be filled with $\frac{3}{4}$ pound of nuts?

   _____ bags can be filled.

7. Jason walked $\frac{5}{6}$ hour. He walked at the rate of 1 mile every $\frac{1}{6}$ hour. How many miles did he walk?

   He walked _____ miles.

8. Suppose in problem 7 Jason walked 1 mile every $\frac{5}{12}$ hour. How many miles did he walk?

   He walked _____ miles.

9. A bell rings every $\frac{1}{6}$ hour. Assume it just rang. How many times will it ring in the next $\frac{2}{3}$ hour?

   It will ring _____ times.

1.
2.
3.
4.
5.
6.
7.
8.
9.

60

Lesson 5 Division

Write each answer in simplest form.

	a	b	c	d
1.	$8 \div \frac{2}{3}$	$\frac{4}{7} \div 5$	$\frac{1}{6} \div \frac{1}{3}$	$\frac{3}{5} \div \frac{2}{3}$
2.	$\frac{1}{8} \div \frac{1}{10}$	$6 \div \frac{1}{4}$	$\frac{1}{3} \div 2$	$\frac{1}{7} \div \frac{1}{3}$
3.	$\frac{1}{2} \div \frac{1}{5}$	$\frac{9}{10} \div \frac{4}{5}$	$9 \div \frac{3}{5}$	$\frac{4}{9} \div 6$
4.	$\frac{3}{5} \div 3$	$\frac{1}{3} \div \frac{1}{6}$	$\frac{3}{8} \div \frac{3}{10}$	$6 \div \frac{4}{5}$
5.	$\frac{7}{8} \div \frac{7}{8}$	$\frac{6}{7} \div \frac{8}{9}$	$7 \div \frac{1}{3}$	$\frac{6}{7} \div 4$

NAME _____

Problem Solving

Solve. Write each answer in simplest form.

1. It takes $\frac{1}{3}$ hour to produce 1 woomble. How many woombles could be produced in 9 hours?

   _____ woombles could be produced.

   1. _____

2. A rope $\frac{3}{4}$ yard long is cut into 9 pieces. Each piece is the same length. How long is each piece?

   Each piece is _____ yard long.

   2. _____

3. Each class period is $\frac{3}{5}$ hour long. How many topics can be covered in 1 class period if it takes $\frac{3}{10}$ hour to cover each topic?

   _____ topics can be covered.

   3. _____

4. Eight pounds of raisins are put in boxes. How many boxes are needed if $\frac{2}{3}$ pound of raisins is put into each box?

   _____ boxes are needed.

   4. _____

5. Michelle and her 5 friends want to share $\frac{3}{4}$ pound of salami equally. How much salami will each person get?

   Each person will get _____ pound.

   5. _____

6. A wire $4\frac{1}{2}$ feet long is cut into 9 pieces of the same length. How long is each piece?

   Each piece is _____ foot long.

   6. _____

7. Three-fourths gallon of milk is poured into 12 glasses. The same amount is in each glass. How much milk is in each glass?

   _____ gallon is in each glass.

   7. _____

8. Mr. Roe has $\frac{9}{10}$ pound of a chemical to put into 6 tubes. Assume he puts the same amount in each tube. How many pounds of chemical will be in each tube?

   _____ pound will be in each tube.

   8. _____

62

Lesson 6 Division

$$2\frac{1}{5} \div 4 = \frac{11}{5} \div 4$$

Change the mixed numerals to fractions.

$$= \frac{11}{5} \times \frac{1}{4}$$

To divide, multiply by the reciprocal.

$$= \frac{11}{20}$$

Multiply the fractions.

Write the answer in simplest form.

$$3\frac{1}{2} \div 1\frac{1}{2} = \frac{7}{2} \div \frac{3}{2}$$

$$= \frac{7}{2} \times \frac{2}{3}$$

$$= \frac{14}{6}$$

$$= 2\frac{1}{3}$$

Write each answer in simplest form.

	a	*b*	*c*	*d*
1.	$2\frac{1}{2} \div 3$	$1\frac{2}{5} \div 3$	$4 \div 1\frac{1}{3}$	$6 \div 1\frac{1}{3}$
2.	$1\frac{2}{7} \div 2\frac{1}{2}$	$1\frac{1}{5} \div 2\frac{2}{3}$	$4\frac{1}{2} \div 1\frac{1}{5}$	$1\frac{4}{5} \div 1\frac{1}{5}$
3.	$1\frac{4}{5} \div \frac{2}{7}$	$\frac{1}{6} \div 1\frac{1}{2}$	$3\frac{3}{5} \div 10$	$1\frac{1}{3} \div 2\frac{1}{2}$

Problem Solving

Solve. Write each answer in simplest form.

1. Five pounds of sand are put into containers. How many containers are needed if $1\frac{1}{4}$ pounds of sand are put into each one?

   _____ containers are needed.

2. Karyln works $1\frac{1}{2}$ hours each day. How many days will it take her to work 15 hours?

   It will take _____ days.

3. Each class period is $\frac{5}{6}$ hour long. How many periods can there be in $2\frac{1}{2}$ hours?

   There can be _____ periods in $2\frac{1}{2}$ hours.

4. The city spread $7\frac{1}{2}$ tons of salt on the streets. There were $1\frac{1}{4}$ tons on each load. How many loads of salt were spread on the streets?

   _____ loads of salt were spread.

5. It takes $1\frac{5}{8}$ hours to assemble a lawn mower. How many lawn mowers could be assembled in $16\frac{1}{2}$ hours?

   _____ lawn mowers could be assembled.

6. How many $1\frac{1}{2}$-hour practice sessions are there in 6 hours?

   There are _____ practice sessions.

7. How many $1\frac{3}{4}$-hour practice sessions are there in $10\frac{1}{2}$ hours?

   There are _____ practice sessions.

1.

2.

3.

4.

5.

6.

7.

64

CHAPTER 5 TEST

Write each answer in simplest form.

| | *a* | *b* | *c* | *d* |

1. $5 \div \dfrac{1}{3}$ $\qquad$ $8 \div \dfrac{3}{4}$ $\qquad$ $4 \div \dfrac{2}{3}$ $\qquad$ $10 \div \dfrac{6}{7}$

2. $\dfrac{1}{2} \div 3$ $\qquad$ $\dfrac{4}{7} \div 3$ $\qquad$ $\dfrac{5}{9} \div 5$ $\qquad$ $\dfrac{6}{7} \div 8$

3. $\dfrac{1}{9} \div \dfrac{1}{4}$ $\qquad$ $\dfrac{1}{10} \div \dfrac{1}{5}$ $\qquad$ $\dfrac{1}{5} \div \dfrac{1}{10}$ $\qquad$ $\dfrac{1}{3} \div \dfrac{1}{4}$

4. $\dfrac{1}{6} \div \dfrac{1}{9}$ $\qquad$ $\dfrac{4}{5} \div \dfrac{3}{4}$ $\qquad$ $\dfrac{7}{9} \div \dfrac{2}{3}$ $\qquad$ $\dfrac{5}{8} \div \dfrac{5}{6}$

5. $2\dfrac{1}{3} \div 5$ $\qquad$ $6 \div 1\dfrac{2}{3}$ $\qquad$ $\dfrac{1}{3} \div 1\dfrac{1}{2}$ $\qquad$ $3\dfrac{1}{3} \div 1\dfrac{1}{2}$

PRE-TEST—Addition and Subtraction

Change each fraction or mixed numeral to a decimal.

a	b	c
1. $\dfrac{7}{10} =$ _____	$3\dfrac{19}{100} =$ _____	$5\dfrac{25}{1000} =$ _____

Change each of the following to a decimal as indicated.

2. Change $\frac{4}{5}$ to tenths.   Change $3\frac{8}{25}$ to hundredths.   Change $3\frac{16}{125}$ to thousandths.

Change each decimal to a fraction or mixed numeral in simplest form.

a	b	c
3. 0.8	9.33	16.125

Add or subtract.

	a	b	c	d
4.	0.6 +0.2	0.7 2 +0.3 5	5.3 8 2 +2.6 4 1	5.0 1 8 3.2 4 6 +5.8 1 2
5.	4.6 −3.5	5.0 5 −4.2 9	0.4 5 6 −0.0 1 8	1 2.0 3 8 −1.7 6 4
6.	0.7 +0.3 8	0.2 5 6 +0.8 3	1.7 +5.8 2 5	3.4 4 2.0 1 8 +0.7 9
7.	0.4 2 −0.1	4.5 6 −1.2 4 3	5.8 −2.2 5	1 6.3 6 −1 6.0 7 5

NAME _____

Lesson 1   Tenths

Numerals like 0.4, 4.1, and 5.4 are called **decimals.**

$\frac{1}{10} = 0.1$ 0.1 is read "one tenth."

$0.4 = \frac{\frac{4}{10}}{}$ $\frac{3}{10} = \underline{0.3}$

decimal
points

$4\frac{1}{10} = 4$ 4.1 is read "four and one tenth." $5.4 = \underline{\hspace{1cm}}$ $2\frac{3}{10} = \underline{\hspace{1cm}}$

Change each fraction or mixed numeral to a decimal.

	a	b	c	d

1. $\frac{6}{10} = \underline{\hspace{1cm}}$ $\frac{2}{10} = \underline{\hspace{1cm}}$ $\frac{8}{10} = \underline{\hspace{1cm}}$ $\frac{5}{10} = \underline{\hspace{1cm}}$

2. $4\frac{7}{10} = \underline{\hspace{1cm}}$ $5\frac{9}{10} = \underline{\hspace{1cm}}$ $18\frac{2}{10} = \underline{\hspace{1cm}}$ $423\frac{6}{10} = \underline{\hspace{1cm}}$

Change each decimal to a fraction or mixed numeral.

3. $0.7 = \underline{\hspace{1cm}}$ $0.3 = \underline{\hspace{1cm}}$ $0.1 = \underline{\hspace{1cm}}$ $0.9 = \underline{\hspace{1cm}}$

4. $4.9 = \underline{\hspace{1cm}}$ $12.7 = \underline{\hspace{1cm}}$ $15.1 = \underline{\hspace{1cm}}$ $217.3 = \underline{\hspace{1cm}}$

Write a decimal for each of the following.

	a		b	

5. eight tenths _____   three and seven tenths   _____

6. four tenths _____   twenty-five and eight tenths   _____

7. five tenths _____   one hundred and six tenths   _____

Write each decimal in words.

8. 0.9 _____

9. 3.7 _____

10. 21.2 _____

67

Lesson 2   Hundredths

$\dfrac{1}{100}$ = 0.01   0.01 is read "one hundredth."

$0.15 = \dfrac{15}{100}$ $\dfrac{9}{100} = 0.09$

$3\dfrac{12}{100}$ = 3.12   3.12 is read
"three and twelve hundredths."   2.07 = _____ $1\dfrac{14}{100}$ = _____

Change each fraction or mixed numeral to a decimal naming hundredths.

	a	*b*	*c*
1.	$\dfrac{8}{100}$ = _____	$\dfrac{16}{100}$ = _____	$\dfrac{5}{100}$ = _____
2.	$1\dfrac{36}{100}$ = _____	$8\dfrac{6}{100}$ = _____	$9\dfrac{12}{100}$ = _____
3.	$12\dfrac{45}{100}$ = _____	$43\dfrac{67}{100}$ = _____	$26\dfrac{4}{100}$ = _____
4.	$142\dfrac{8}{100}$ = _____	$436\dfrac{42}{100}$ = _____	$389\dfrac{89}{100}$ = _____

Change each decimal to a fraction or mixed numeral.

5.   0.17 = _____   0.03 = _____   0.41 = _____

6.   5.19 = _____   6.47 = _____   5.01 = _____

7.   21.07 = _____   23.99 = _____   44.89 = _____

8. 142.33 = _____   483.03 = _____   185.63 = _____

Write a decimal for each of the following.

	a		*b*
9.	eight hundredths _____	six and twenty-three hundredths	_____
10.	ninety-five hundredths _____	fourteen and sixty hundredths	_____
11.	forty-eight hundredths _____	four and forty-four hundredths	_____

Lesson 3   Thousandths, Ten-Thousandths

$\dfrac{1}{1000} = 0.001$ ◄— one thousandth $\dfrac{1}{10000} = 0.0001$ ◄—— one ten-thousandth

$2\dfrac{12}{1000} = 2.012$ ◄— two and twelve thousandths $1\dfrac{35}{10000} = 1.0035$ ◄—— one and thirty-five ten-thousandths

---

Write each fraction or mixed numeral as a decimal.

	a	*b*	*c*
1.	$\dfrac{8}{1000} =$ _____	$\dfrac{17}{1000} =$ _____	$\dfrac{54}{10000} =$ _____
2.	$\dfrac{125}{10000} =$ _____	$\dfrac{430}{1000} =$ _____	$\dfrac{306}{10000} =$ _____
3.	$4\dfrac{4}{1000} =$ _____	$3\dfrac{41}{10000} =$ _____	$6\dfrac{183}{1000} =$ _____
4.	$35\dfrac{78}{10000} =$ _____	$42\dfrac{19}{1000} =$ _____	$196\dfrac{6}{1000} =$ _____

Write each decimal as a fraction or as a mixed numeral.

	a	*b*	*c*
5.	0.009 = _____	0.0019 = _____	0.0003 = _____
6.	0.123 = _____	0.0441 – _____	0.219 = _____
7.	4.011 = _____	2.1011 = _____	6.0014 = _____
8.	36.037 = _____	3.433 = _____	100.0001 = _____

Write a decimal for each of the following.

	a		*b*	
9.	fifty-three thousandths	_____	ten and nine ten-thousandths	_____
10.	eleven ten-thousandths	_____	twelve and eighteen thousandths	_____
11.	sixty-five thousandths	_____	twelve and one thousandth	_____

Lesson 4 Fractions to Decimals

Change $\frac{1}{2}$ to tenths.

$$\frac{1}{2} = \frac{1}{2} \times \frac{5}{5}$$
$$= \frac{5}{10}$$
$$= 0.5$$

Change $\frac{1}{2}$ to hundredths.

$$\frac{1}{2} = \frac{1}{2} \times \frac{50}{50}$$
$$= \frac{50}{100}$$
$$= 0.50$$

Change $\frac{1}{2}$ to thousandths.

$$\frac{1}{2} = \frac{1}{2} \times \frac{500}{500}$$
$$= \frac{500}{1000}$$
$$= 0.500$$

Change $\frac{3}{4}$ to hundredths.

$$\frac{3}{4} = \frac{3}{4} \times \frac{25}{25}$$
$$= \frac{75}{100}$$

$$= \underline{\hspace{1cm}}$$

Change $3\frac{48}{250}$ to thousandths.

$$3\frac{48}{250} = 3 + \frac{48}{250}$$
$$= 3 + \left(\frac{48}{250} \times \frac{4}{4}\right)$$
$$= 3 + \frac{192}{1000}$$
$$= 3\frac{192}{1000}$$

$$= \underline{\hspace{1cm}}$$

Change each of the following to a decimal as indicated.

| *a* | *b* | *c* |

1. Change $\frac{3}{5}$ to tenths. Change $\frac{3}{5}$ to hundredths. Change $\frac{3}{5}$ to thousandths.

2. Change $3\frac{1}{2}$ to tenths. Change $\frac{7}{25}$ to hundredths. Change $2\frac{19}{100}$ to thousandths.

3. Change $2\frac{4}{5}$ to tenths. Change $\frac{7}{20}$ to hundredths. Change $\frac{7}{125}$ to thousandths.

4. Change $2\frac{1}{5}$ to tenths. Change $\frac{19}{50}$ to hundredths. Change $\frac{88}{250}$ to thousandths.

Lesson 5 Decimals to Fractions

$0.7 = \frac{7}{10}$ $0.6 = \frac{6}{10}$ or $\frac{3}{5}$ $4.2 = 4\frac{2}{10}$ or $4\frac{1}{5}$

$0.19 = \frac{19}{100}$ $0.14 = \frac{14}{100}$ or $\frac{7}{50}$ $3.01 = 3\frac{1}{100}$

$0.051 =$ _____ $0.114 = \frac{114}{1000}$ or _____ $5.006 = 5\frac{6}{1000}$ or _____

Change each decimal to a fraction or mixed numeral in simplest form.

	a	b	c	d
1.	0.3	0.1	0.4	0.5
2.	2.7	3.3	7.2	5.8
3.	0.17	0.03	0.15	0.80
4.	5.07	8.43	4.05	2.44
5.	0.003	0.017	0.125	0.045
6.	3.121	2.987	4.250	3.008
7.	4.35	0.7	6.200	1.007
8.	2.6	3.24	0.250	3.5
9.	5.125	0.9	2.4	0.04
10.	0.01	0.051	0.8	2.19

Lesson 6 Fractions and Decimals

Change each of the following to a decimal as indicated.

	a	*b*	*c*
1.	Change $\frac{1}{5}$ to tenths.	Change $\frac{7}{20}$ to hundredths.	Change $\frac{89}{200}$ to thousandths.

2. Change $7\frac{1}{2}$ to tenths.   Change $4\frac{29}{50}$ to hundredths.   Change $3\frac{9}{25}$ to thousandths.

Change each decimal to a fraction or mixed numeral in simplest form.

	a	*b*	*c*	*d*
3.	0.9	3.6	0.35	17.75
4.	0.025	8.445	24.305	8.05

Complete the following so the numerals in each row name the same number.

	fractions or mixed numerals	decimals		
		tenths	hundredths	thousandths
5.				0.600
6.			2.70	
7.		5.4		
8.	$3\frac{1}{2}$			
9.		17.9		
10.			80.80	

Lesson 7   Addition

When adding decimals, line up the decimal points.
Add decimals like you add whole numbers.

$$\begin{array}{r} 0.6 \\ +0.7 \\ \hline 1.3 \end{array}$$

$$\begin{array}{r} 3.5\overset{1}{}6 \\ 0.0\;3 \\ +4.2\;4 \\ \hline 7.8\;3 \end{array}$$

$$\begin{array}{r} 3.0\;\overset{1}{1}\;8 \\ 0.1\;4\;2 \\ +1\;4.0\;0\;9 \\ \hline 1\;7.1\;6\;9 \end{array}$$

— Place the decimal point in the answer. —

Add.

	a	b	c	d	e
1.	0.4 +0.5	0.9 +0.8	3.4 +9.2	1 9.3 +1 2.8	4 5.6 + 6.8
2.	0. 4 2 +0. 3 5	0.7 6 +0.4 8	3.3 2 +4.6 2	2 4.4 5 +7 2.3 6	5 8.9 2 +3.2 9
3.	0.0 1 4 +0.2 3 1	0.4 5 6 +0.8 7 6	2.0 1 4 +2.3 2 5	3.4 5 7 +2.3 5 6	4 1.2 1 6 +2.0 0 7
4.	0.5 0.6 +0.7	1.9 2.2 +3.4	3.4 1.7 +4.8	4 2.3 1.6 +2.9	3.4 0.8 +4.2
5.	0.3 3 0.2 6 +0.4 1	$0.4 3 0.5 4 +0.0 7	3.3 5 1.0 8 +6.1 1	$2 4.2 9 1 2.2 9 +5.3 1	$3 4.0 5 2.0 6 +1.0 8
6.	0.0 1 2 0.3 0 4 +0.4 0 5	0.4 2 3 0.0 5 6 +0.2 1 7	3.0 5 6 1.4 5 2 +6.1 1 2	4.0 0 8 2.3 0 9 +0.0 1 2	3 5.1 5 7 0.4 4 8 +2.5 0 9

73

Problem Solving

Solve each problem.

1. There was 0.8 inch of rain recorded on Monday, 0.5 inch on Tuesday, and 0.7 inch on Friday. How many inches of rain were recorded on those 3 days?

   _____ inches were recorded.

1. _____

2. In problem **1**, how many inches of rain were recorded on Monday and Friday?

   _____ inches were recorded.

2. _____

3. A board is 4.25 meters long. Another is 3.75 meters long. When laid end to end, the boards are how long?

   The boards are _____ meters long.

3. _____

4. One sheet of metal is 0.28 centimeter thick. Another is 0.35 centimeter thick. What would be the combined thickness of these sheets?

   The thickness would be _____ centimeter.

4. _____

5. Three sheets of metal are to be placed on top of each other. Their thicknesses are 0.125 inch, 0.018 inch, and 0.075 inch. What would be the combined thickness of all three pieces?

   The combined thickness would be _____ inch.

5. _____

6. Box A weighs 1.4 pounds, box B weighs 3.2 pounds, and box C weighs 2.5 pounds. What is the combined weight of box A and box C?

   The combined weight is _____ pounds.

6. _____

7. In problem 6, what is the combined weight of all three boxes?

   The combined weight is _____ pounds.

7. _____

8. Spencer made three purchases at the store. The amounts were $13.75; $1.42; and $0.83. What was the total amount of all three purchases?

   The total amount was $_____ .

8. _____

Lesson 8   Addition

You may write these 0's
if they help you add.

```
                                    4.2          4.2 0 0
  0.8        0.8 0              3.0 1 8   or   3.0 1 8
+0.3 9  or  +0.3 9             +0.8 2         +0.8 2 0
 1.1 9       1.1 9             8.0 3 8         8.0 3 8
```

Add. If necessary, use 0's as shown in the examples.

	a	*b*	*c*	*d*	*e*
1.	0.9 +0.4 2	0.8 3 +0.4	0.6 +0.4 0 1	0.7 2 +0.4 2 3	0.6 4 5 +0.2
2.	2.7 5 +3.3 0 8	5.5 4 +7.6	3.8 +0.3 1 6	0.2 9 +8.0 4 3	2 9.5 + 4.9 3
3.	0.4 2 0.8 +0.0 1 8	0.3 1 0.2 +0.4 5	0.7 6 0.8 2 +0.9	0.4 3 1 0.2 +0.4 5	0.5 0.3 1 6 +0.0 9 9
4.	3.1 8 2 1.3 4 1 2.6	4.7 2 5.8 +6.3 1 7	7.4 2 6 3.3 1 8 +0.2	0.7 3 1 8.4 5 1 2.2 8	0.3 0.3 8 4 +9.4 2

Complete the following.

a	*b*

5. 0.8 + 0.91 = _____   0.4 + 0.016 + 0.75 = _____

6. 0.58 + 0.114 = _____   0.32 + 0.42 + 0.113 = _____

7. 0.9 + 0.301 = _____   4.8 + 3.21 + 0.014 = _____

8. 2.4 + 0.31 = _____   5.24 + 0.016 + 21.3 = _____

Problem Solving

Solve each problem.

1. There was 0.75 inch of rain recorded at Elmhurst, 0.50 inch at River Forest, and 0.25 inch at Harvey. What amount of rain was recorded at both Elmhurst and River Forest?

   The amount at both was _____ inches of rain.

2. In problem **1**, how much rain was recorded at all three locations?

   _____ inches were recorded.

3. An opening in an engine part is supposed to be 1.150 centimeters. The part is acceptable if the opening is as much as 0.075 centimeter larger than what it is supposed to be. What is the largest opening that would be acceptable?

   The largest opening is _____ centimeters.

4. Assume the opening in problem 3 can only be as much as 0.025 centimeter larger than what it is supposed to be. What is the largest acceptable opening?

   The largest opening is _____ centimeters.

5. Andy saved $23.05. Sarah saved $40. Jenna saved $3.50. How much have all three saved?

   All three have saved a total of _____ .

6. In problem 5, how much have Andy and Jenna saved?

   They have saved _____ .

7. In problem 5, how much have Sarah and Jenna saved?

   They have saved _____ .

8. Marlene was asked to find the sum of 1.9; 3.52; and 0.075. What should her answer be?

   Her answer should be _____ .

1.

2.

3.

4.

5.

6.

7.

8.

Lesson 9   Subtraction

When subtracting decimals, line up the decimal points. Subtract decimals like you subtract whole numbers.

$$
\begin{array}{r} 9.5 \\ -2.3 \\ \hline 7.2 \end{array}
\qquad
\begin{array}{r} \overset{3\ 13}{4.\cancel{3}} \\ -1.6 \\ \hline 2.7 \end{array}
\qquad
\begin{array}{r} \overset{0\ 14}{0.1\,\cancel{4}} \\ -0.0\ 8 \\ \hline 0.0\ 6 \end{array}
\qquad
\begin{array}{r} \overset{3\ 12\quad 4\ 13}{\cancel{4}\ 2.7\ \cancel{5}\ \cancel{3}} \\ -5.3\ 2\ 7 \\ \hline 3\ 7.4\ 2\ 6 \end{array}
$$

Place the decimal point in the answer.

Subtract.

	a	b	c	d	e
1.	0.7 −0.3	0.9 −0.2	0.6 −0.2	0.9 −0.1	0.8 −0.5
2.	0.4 2 −0.3 1	0.5 6 −0.2 3	0.0 7 −0.0 2	0.8 5 −0.3 7	$0.5 2 −0.3 7
3.	0.3 4 5 −0.2 3 4	0.5 4 8 −0.2 5 9	0.8 1 5 −0.6 0 7	0.8 2 8 −0.3 8 9	0.7 5 4 −0.3 7 5
4.	4.6 −3.2	7.4 −2.8	8.6 −3.7	5.6 −0.7	1 9.2 −0.9
5.	4.3 6 −1.2 3	$6.5 5 −2.7 3	4.0 8 −0.3 9	$1 5.3 2 −2.6 7	$ 4.0 9 −0.3 2
6.	4.2 1 3 −2.0 0 1	3.6 2 4 −1.4 1 5	4.3 0 7 −1.4 9 5	26.3 4 5 −2.5 4 3	15.1 0 8 −3.9 1 2
7.	1 5.3 −4.9	6.2 3 −3.7 5	14.2 1 −7.0 8	3.0 0 2 −1.0 4 7	19.8 0 1 −7.4 1 3

Problem Solving

Solve each problem.

1. Katie is to mix 0.8 pound of chemical A, 0.6 pound of chemical B, and 0.3 pound of chemical C. How much more of chemical A is to be used than chemical B?

    _____ pound more of chemical A is to be used.

2. In problem 1, how much more of chemical A than chemical C is to be used?

    _____ pound more of chemical A is to be used.

3. A spark plug has a gap of 1.12 millimeters. The gap should be 0.89 millimeter. How much too large is the gap?

    It is _____ millimeter too large.

4. Suppose the gap in problem 3 was 0.65 millimeter. How much too small is the gap?

    It is _____ millimeter too small.

5. Three sheets of metal were placed together. Their total thickness was 4.525 inches. Then a sheet 1.750 inches thick was removed. What was the combined thickness of the remaining sheets?

    It was _____ inches thick.

6. The distance between two terminals on a television part is supposed to be 2.45 inches. The part is acceptable if the distance is 0.05 inches more or less than what it is supposed to be. What is the least distance that would be acceptable?

    The least distance would be _____ inches.

7. One box of nails weighs 3.4 pounds and another box weighs 5.2 pounds. How much more does the heavier box weigh?

    The heavier box weighs _____ pounds more.

1.
2.
3.
4.
5.
6.
7.

Lesson 10   Subtraction

$$\begin{array}{r}\overset{5\ 14}{6.4\cancel{4}3\ 2}\\ -1.7\quad\quad\\\hline 4.7\ 3\ 2\end{array}\ \text{or}\ \begin{array}{r}\overset{5\ 14}{6.4\cancel{4}3\ 2}\\ -1.7\ 0\ 0\\\hline 4.7\ 3\ 2\end{array}$$ ←—Write these 0's if they help you.

$$\begin{array}{r}6.4\\ -1.2\ 3\end{array}\ \rightarrow\ \begin{array}{r}\overset{3\ 10}{6.4\cancel{0}}\\ -1.2\ 3\\\hline 5.1\ 7\end{array}$$ ←— Write this 0 to help you subtract.

Subtract.

	a	b	c	d	e
1.	0.7 2 −0.2	3.5 6 −1.4	5.3 8 −2.7	4.3 1 6 −1.1	2.1 4 6 −1.5
2.	0.5 2 3 −0.4 1	0.683 −0.39	5.4 2 1 −0.5 6	3.0 1 8 −0.2 7	4.0 1 2 −3.0 3
3.	0.8 −0.3 5	0.5 −0.2 6	6.3 −1.1 2	7.4 −2.7 5	1 4.3 −6.7 2
4.	0.9 −0.3 0 9	0.3 −0.1 7 5	4.4 −2.3 5 6	6.3 3.4 3 2	1 8.2 −7.5 1 4
5.	0.7 5 −0.3 1 4	0.3 6 −0.2 7 5	5.7 2 −1.3 1 2	4.3 8 −0.5 9 2	1 6.9 2 −6.3 8 4
6.	3 4.2 6 5 −2.1 8	42.1 6 −3.2 3 5	4 2.2 −3.1 6 4	2 6.3 −2.4 5	3.1 0 6 −2.0 3
7.	4 3.7 −6.1 8	3 9 4.6 −7 5.8 1	5.2 1 6 −4.1 9	8 2.4 5 −3.7 8 3	9 2.4 0 5 −3.0 0 8

Problem Solving

Today's Work Report		
Ms. Williams	14.7 units	1.2 hours
Mr. Karns	8.4 units	0.9 hour
Mr. Anders	13.5 units	1.4 hours

The manufacturing director uses her computer to find out how many units her workers are producing. Use the information above to solve each problem.

1. How many more units did Ms. Williams make than Mr. Anders?

Ms. Williams made _____ more units.

2. Who made the most units? Who made the fewest units? What is the difference between the most and the fewest units made?

_____ made the most units.

_____ made the fewest units.

The difference is _____ units.

3. How many units did the three workers make in all?

The three workers made _____ units.

4. How long did the three workers work on the units in all?

The three workers worked _____ hours.

1.

2.

3.

4.

CHAPTER 6 TEST

Change each fraction or mixed numeral to a decimal.

	a	b	c
1.	$\dfrac{175}{1000} = $ _____	$9\dfrac{4}{10} = $ _____	$3\dfrac{8}{100} = $ _____

Change each of the following to a decimal as indicated.

2.   Change $\frac{9}{10}$ to hundredths.   Change $3\frac{1}{5}$ to tenths.   Change $5\frac{75}{250}$ to thousandths.

Change each decimal to a fraction or mixed numeral in simplest form.

	a	b	c
3.	0.075	8.6	16.49

Add or subtract.

	a	b	c	d
4.	0.9 +0.4	0.5 2 +0.4 3	6.5 3 4 +7.8 2 7	9.3 0 8 2 1.2 9 5 +0.0 4 3
5.	3.3 −1.6	8.2 4 −3.7 3	0.4 4 2 −0.3 7 5	1 8.0 4 2 −1 2.3 4 5
6.	0.4 2 +0.9	0.3 5 +0.0 6 5	3.6 +1 4.6 7 3	9.2 4.3 7 5 +4 3.7 8
7.	0.5 4 6 −0.3 8	3.8 −1.2 1	7.2 2 −4.4 3 6	8.4 −3.5 7 5

PRE-TEST—Multiplication

Multiply.

	a	b	c	d	e
1.	0.7 ×5	0.4 ×2	4 ×0.9	4 ×0.3	5 ×0.6
2.	0.0 7 ×6	0.0 2 ×3	8 ×0.0 4	8 ×0.0 9	5 ×0.0 8
3.	0.0 0 3 ×4	0.0 0 1 ×8	2 ×0.0 0 3	4 ×0.0 0 1	6 ×0.0 0 2
4.	0.7 ×0.3	0.2 ×0.4	0.4 ×0.6	0.9 ×0.6	0.8 ×0.5
5.	0.0 6 ×0.8	0.0 1 ×0.5	0.2 ×0.0 3	0.0 6 ×0.0 7	0.0 2 ×0.0 2
6.	0.4 ×1 0	0.0 0 8 ×1 0 0	6.7 2 ×1 0	0.2 3 4 ×1 0 0 0	5.6 8 ×1 0 0 0
7.	1 6 ×0.3	0.4 7 ×0.5	3.4 ×0.0 8	5.0 1 ×0.2 5	0.0 7 8 ×7.5

Lesson 1   Multiplication

number of digits to the right of the
decimal point

4	0	0.4	1	0.04	2	0.04	2	0.04	2
×3	+0	×3	+0	× 3	+0	× .3	+1	×.03	+2
12	0	1.2	1	0.12	2	0.012	3	0.0012	4

Write in as many 0's as needed to
place the decimal point correctly.

Multiply.

	a	b	c	d	e
1.	2 ×3	0.2 ×3	0.0 2 ×3	0.0 0 2 ×3	2 ×0.3
2.	8 ×6	0.8 ×6	0.0 8 ×6	0.0 0 8 ×6	0.0 6 ×8
3.	5 ×3	0.5 ×3	0.0 5 ×3	0.0 0 5 ×3	0.0 0 3 ×5
4.	3 ×4	0.3 ×0.4	0.0 3 ×0.4	0. 0 4 ×0.3	0.0 3 ×0.0 4
5.	6 ×7	0.6 ×0.7	0.0 6 ×0.7	0.0 7 ×0.6	0.0 6 ×0.0 7
6.	9 ×8	0.9 ×0.8	0.0 9 ×0.8	0.0 8 ×0.9	0.0 9 ×0.0 8

Lesson 2   Multiplication

number of digits to the right of the
decimal point

24	0	2.4	1	0.24	2	0.24	2	0.24	2
×36	+0	×36	+0	×36	+0	×3.6	+1	×0.36	+2
864	0	86.4	1	8.64	2	0.864	3	0.0864	4

Use the completed multiplication to find each product.

		a	b	c	d
1.	32 ×14 448	3.2 ×1 4	0.3 2 ×1 4	0.3 2 ×1.4	0.3 2 ×0.1 4
2.	27 ×48 1,296	2.7 ×4 8	0.2 7 ×4 8	0.2 7 ×4.8	0.2 7 ×0.4 8
3.	26 ×34 884	0.2 6 ×3 4	0.2 6 ×3.4	0.2 6 ×0.3 4	2.6 ×3 4
4.	74 ×26 1,924	0.7 4 ×2.6	7.4 ×2 6	0.7 4 ×2 6	0.7 4 ×0.2 6
5.	25 ×3 75	2 5 ×0.3	2.5 ×0.0 3	2 5 ×0.03	0.2 5 ×0.0 3
6.	12 ×4 48	1.2 ×0.4	0.1 2 ×4	0.1 2 ×0.4	0.1 2 ×0.0 4
7.	73 ×3 219	7 3 ×0.0 3	0.7 3 ×0.0 3	7.3 ×0.3	0.7 3 ×0.3

Lesson 3 Multiplication

6	0.6	0.6	0.06	0.06	0.06	0.006
×3	×3	×0.3	× 3	×0.3	×0.03	×0.3
18	1.8	0.18	0.18	0.018	0.0018	0.0018

Multiply.

	a	b	c	d	e
1.	0.7 ×5	3 ×0.2	0.8 ×9	7 ×0.3	0.2 ×4
2.	0.8 ×0.6	0.1 ×0.6	0.3 ×0.7	0.2 ×0.4	0.7 ×0.6
3.	0.0 8 ×4	0.0 2 ×3	7 ×0.0 8	0.0 9 ×6	5 ×0.0 3
4.	0.0 5 ×0.9	0.7 ×0.0 5	0.0 8 ×0.8	0.2 ×0.0 3	0.0 3 ×0.5
5.	0.0 3 ×0.0 8	0.0 4 ×0.0 6	0.0 9 ×0.0 1	0.0 7 ×0.0 8	0.0 3 ×0.02
6.	0.0 0 7 ×9	6 ×0.0 0 8	0.0 0 4 ×6	0.0 0 8 ×4	5 ×0.0 0 7
7.	0.0 0 5 ×0.9	0.0 0 9 ×0.9	0.3 ×0.0 0 4	0.0 0 3 ×0.3	0.5 ×0.0 0 5

NAME _____

Lesson 4   Multiplication

			Shortcut

$$\begin{array}{r} 2.51 \\ \times 10 \\ \hline 25.10 \end{array} \qquad \begin{array}{r} 2.51 \\ \times 100 \\ \hline 251.00 \end{array} \qquad \begin{array}{r} 2.51 \\ \times 1000 \\ \hline 2510.00 \end{array}$$

or   or   or

25.1   251   2,510

$2.51 \times 10 = 2.5.1$

$2.51 \times 100 = 2.51$

$2.51 \times 1000 = 2.510$

$$\begin{array}{r} 0.085 \\ \times 10 \\ \hline 0.850 \end{array} \qquad \begin{array}{r} 0.085 \\ \times 100 \\ \hline 8.500 \end{array} \qquad \begin{array}{r} 0.085 \\ \times 1000 \\ \hline 85.000 \end{array}$$

or   or   or

0.85   8.5   85

$0.085 \times 10 = 0.85$

$0.085 \times 100 = 08.5$

$0.085 \times 1000 = 085$

Multiply.

	a	*b*	*c*	*d*	*e*
1.	$\begin{array}{r} 5.6\,4\,2 \\ \times 1\,0 \\ \hline \end{array}$	$\begin{array}{r} 5.6\,4\,2 \\ \times 1\,0\,0 \\ \hline \end{array}$	$\begin{array}{r} 5.6\,4\,2 \\ \times 1\,0\,0\,0 \\ \hline \end{array}$	$\begin{array}{r} 5\,6.4\,2 \\ \times 1\,0\,0 \\ \hline \end{array}$	$\begin{array}{r} 0.5\,6\,4\,2 \\ \times 1\,0 \\ \hline \end{array}$
2.	$\begin{array}{r} 0.1\,0\,6\,4 \\ \times 1\,0 \\ \hline \end{array}$	$\begin{array}{r} 0.1\,0\,6\,4 \\ \times 1\,0\,0 \\ \hline \end{array}$	$\begin{array}{r} 0.1\,0\,6\,4 \\ \times 1\,0\,0\,0 \\ \hline \end{array}$	$\begin{array}{r} 0.0\,1\,0\,6 \\ \times 1\,0 \\ \hline \end{array}$	$\begin{array}{r} 1.0\,6\,4 \\ \times 1\,0\,0\,0 \\ \hline \end{array}$
3.	$\begin{array}{r} 0.2\,3 \\ \times 1\,0 \\ \hline \end{array}$	$\begin{array}{r} 0.2\,3 \\ \times 1\,0\,0 \\ \hline \end{array}$	$\begin{array}{r} 0.2\,3 \\ \times 1\,0\,0\,0 \\ \hline \end{array}$	$\begin{array}{r} 0.0\,2\,3 \\ \times 1\,0 \\ \hline \end{array}$	$\begin{array}{r} 0.0\,0\,2\,3 \\ \times 1\,0\,0 \\ \hline \end{array}$
4.	$\begin{array}{r} 0.0\,0\,8 \\ \times 1\,0 \\ \hline \end{array}$	$\begin{array}{r} 0.0\,0\,8 \\ \times 1\,0\,0 \\ \hline \end{array}$	$\begin{array}{r} 0.0\,0\,8 \\ \times 1\,0\,0\,0 \\ \hline \end{array}$	$\begin{array}{r} 0.0\,8 \\ \times 1\,0\,0 \\ \hline \end{array}$	$\begin{array}{r} 0.0\,8 \\ \times 1\,0\,0\,0 \\ \hline \end{array}$
5.	$\begin{array}{r} 1.5 \\ \times 1\,0 \\ \hline \end{array}$	$\begin{array}{r} 1.5 \\ \times 1\,0\,0 \\ \hline \end{array}$	$\begin{array}{r} 1.5 \\ \times 1\,0\,0\,0 \\ \hline \end{array}$	$\begin{array}{r} 1\,5 \\ \times 1\,0\,0 \\ \hline \end{array}$	$\begin{array}{r} 0.1\,5 \\ \times 1\,0 \\ \hline \end{array}$

Lesson 5 Multiplication

	Multiply as whole numbers.	Place the decimal point in the product.

$$\begin{array}{r} 0.356 \\ \times 4.2 \\ \hline \end{array} \longrightarrow \begin{array}{r} 0.356 \\ \times 4.2 \\ \hline 712 \\ 1424 \\ \hline 14952 \end{array} \longrightarrow \begin{array}{r} 0.356 \\ \times 4.2 \\ \hline 712 \\ 1424 \\ \hline 1.4952 \end{array}$$

Multiply.

1.

$$\begin{array}{r} 4\,3 \\ \times 0.0\,8 \\ \hline \end{array} \qquad \begin{array}{r} 5.4 \\ \times 0.0\,4 \\ \hline \end{array} \qquad \begin{array}{r} 0.0\,7\,6 \\ \times 0.7 \\ \hline \end{array} \qquad \begin{array}{r} 0.1\,8 \\ \times 0.0\,9 \\ \hline \end{array} \qquad \begin{array}{r} 0.0\,9\,2 \\ \times 8 \\ \hline \end{array}$$

2.

$$\begin{array}{r} 0.1\,3\,7 \\ \times 0.3 \\ \hline \end{array} \qquad \begin{array}{r} 4.8\,2 \\ \times 8 \\ \hline \end{array} \qquad \begin{array}{r} 9\,0\,7 \\ \times 0.4 \\ \hline \end{array} \qquad \begin{array}{r} 6.5\,3 \\ \times 0.7 \\ \hline \end{array} \qquad \begin{array}{r} 0.4\,1\,6 \\ \times 6 \\ \hline \end{array}$$

3.

$$\begin{array}{r} 3\,2.1 \\ \times 0.5 \\ \hline \end{array} \qquad \begin{array}{r} 5.0\,6 \\ \times 4 \\ \hline \end{array} \qquad \begin{array}{r} 0.0\,7\,0\,9 \\ \times 4 \\ \hline \end{array} \qquad \begin{array}{r} 0.4\,2\,1 \\ \times 0.2 \\ \hline \end{array} \qquad \begin{array}{r} 0.0\,5\,0\,3 \\ \times 9 \\ \hline \end{array}$$

4.

$$\begin{array}{r} 0.2\,7 \\ \times 4.2 \\ \hline \end{array} \qquad \begin{array}{r} 5.8 \\ \times 0.1\,6 \\ \hline \end{array} \qquad \begin{array}{r} 0.0\,3 \\ \times 2.5 \\ \hline \end{array} \qquad \begin{array}{r} 0.\,4\,2 \\ \times 0.5\,3 \\ \hline \end{array} \qquad \begin{array}{r} 7.6 \\ \times 7.6 \\ \hline \end{array}$$

5.

$$\begin{array}{r} 0.1\,8\,7 \\ \times 3.5 \\ \hline \end{array} \qquad \begin{array}{r} 0.0\,8\,4 \\ \times 42 \\ \hline \end{array} \qquad \begin{array}{r} 1\,6.1 \\ \times 5.3 \\ \hline \end{array} \qquad \begin{array}{r} 0.0\,7\,2 \\ \times 6.2 \\ \hline \end{array} \qquad \begin{array}{r} 5.2\,1 \\ \times 0.7\,5 \\ \hline \end{array}$$

6.

$$\begin{array}{r} 4\,2.1\,6 \\ \times 1.8 \\ \hline \end{array} \qquad \begin{array}{r} 0.4\,2\,1\,8 \\ \times 22 \\ \hline \end{array} \qquad \begin{array}{r} 3\,0\,6.4 \\ \times 0.2\,4 \\ \hline \end{array} \qquad \begin{array}{r} 0.0\,3\,1\,4 \\ \times 2\,6 \\ \hline \end{array} \qquad \begin{array}{r} 0.0\,1\,4\,4 \\ \times 3\,7 \\ \hline \end{array}$$

Problem Solving

Solve each problem.

1. A box of seeds weighs 0.9 pound. How many pounds would 6 boxes weigh?

   They would weigh _____ pounds.

2. A machinist has 4 sheets of metal, each 0.042 inch thick. These are placed one on top of the other. What is the total thickness of the sheets?

   It will be _____ inch thick.

3. Each needle weighs 0.03 gram. How many grams would 100 needles weigh?

   They would weigh _____ grams.

4. A log weighs 42.1 kilograms. How much would 0.5 of the log weigh?

   It would weigh _____ kilograms.

5. The thickness of a sheet of plastic is 0.024 inch. What would be the combined thickness of 6 sheets of plastic?

   The combined thickness would be _____ inch.

6. In problem 5, what would be the combined thickness of 8 sheets of plastic?

   The combined thickness would be _____ inch.

7. Mrs. Tomasello has 92 sheets of foil. Each sheet is 0.0413 inch thick. What is the combined thickness of the sheets?

   The combined thickness is _____ inches.

8. Mr. McClean's car averages 5.7 kilometers per liter of gasoline. How many kilometers would he be able to travel with 84 liters of gasoline?

   He could travel _____ kilometers.

9. Suppose the car in problem 8 averages 4.9 kilometers per liter. How far could the car go on 84 liters of gasoline?

   It could go _____ kilometers.

1.	2.
3.	4.
5.	6.
7.	8.
9.	

88

Lesson 6 Multiplication

Multiply.

	a	*b*	*c*	*d*
1.	0.6 ×0.4	0.0 8 ×9	0.0 7 ×0.0 7	0.0 0 5 ×8
2.	4.5 ×0.2 7	0.3 8 ×0.3 2	2.6 ×0.0 4 3	7.5 ×2.5
3.	0.1 4 9 ×5 3	4 7.6 ×0.0 4 2	3.0 8 ×5.3	0.7 2 9 ×6.1
4.	3 5.4 6 ×0.2 7	3 1 8.2 ×0.3 6	9.8 0 4 ×2 6	8 0 0.6 ×0.0 4 3
5.	7.2 1 ×5.3 4	4 0.7 ×4.3 1	3 1 2 ×0.0 6 2 4	0.5 9 8 ×7 5.3

Problem Solving

Solve each problem.

1. Each box of bolts weighs 1.7 pounds. There are 24 boxes in a carton. How many pounds would a carton of bolts weigh?

   A carton would weigh _____ pounds.

2. A sheet of paper is 0.012 centimeter thick. How many centimeters thick would a stack of paper be if it contained 28 sheets of paper?

   The stack would be _____ centimeter thick.

3. Each sheet of metal is 0.024 centimeter thick. There are 67 sheets of metal in a stack. How high is the stack?

   The stack is _____ centimeters high.

4. Mrs. Washington's car averaged 18.36 miles per gallon of gasoline. She bought 11.25 gallons of gasoline. How many miles can she travel on that amount of gasoline?

   She can travel _____ miles.

5. After a tune-up, Mrs. Washington's car averaged 21.78 miles per gallon of gasoline. How many miles can she travel on 11.25 gallons of gasoline?

   She can travel _____ miles.

6. Each container filled with chemical X weighs 32.7 pounds. How many pounds would 100 containers weigh?

   They would weigh _____ pounds.

7. To make each unit takes 0.035 hour. How long will it take to make 224 units?

   It will take _____ hours.

8. Suppose a new machine can make each unit in 0.018 hour. How long will that machine take to make 224 units?

   It will take _____ hours.

1.	2.
3.	4.
5.	6.
7.	8.

CHAPTER 7 TEST

Multiply.

	a	*b*	*c*	*d*	*e*
1.	0.6 ×0.8	0.1 8 ×7	0.3 0 8 ×0.9	0.4 2 ×5.3	1.7 3 ×2.8
2.	9 ×0.6	2.4 ×0.3	4 2.6 ×0.7	0.6 4 ×0.7 5	1 4 6 ×0.5 2
3.	0.0 5 ×0.3	0.6 4 ×0.9	3.1 5 ×0.9	5.8 ×6.1	3 5.6 ×0.4 2
4.	4 ×0.0 2	5.3 ×0.0 4	6.0 2 ×0.0 4	7.8 1 ×1 5.2	0.1 6 2 8 ×1 0 0
5.	0.9 ×0.0 0 6	0.6 7 ×0.0 2	5 3 2 ×0.0 7	3.8 6 ×4.0 4	4 1 8 ×0.6 3 2

PRE-TEST—Division

Divide.

	a	b	c	d

1. $2\overline{)14.6}$ $7\overline{)1.89}$ $9\overline{)0.405}$ $6\overline{)0.0114}$

2. $0.3\overline{)6}$ $0.5\overline{)75}$ $0.02\overline{)42}$ $0.004\overline{)16}$

3. $0.6\overline{)0.72}$ $0.3\overline{)6.3}$ $0.04\overline{)0.096}$ $0.003\overline{)0.015}$

4. $0.04\overline{)3.2}$ $0.08\overline{)4.8}$ $0.002\overline{)7.26}$ $0.003\overline{)1.8}$

5. $0.18\overline{)27}$ $1.7\overline{)0.238}$ $4.6\overline{)2.116}$ $0.38\overline{)0.3496}$

8

Lesson 1 Division

Place a decimal point in the quotient directly above the decimal point in the dividend. Then divide as if both numbers were whole numbers.

```
      17              1.7             0.17            0.017
6) 102          6) 10.2         6) 1.02         6) 0.102
   60              60              60              60
   42              42              42              42
   42              42              42              42
    0               0               0               0
```

Divide.

	a	b	c	d	e

1. 4) 2 9 2   4) 2 9.2   4) 2.9 2   4) 0. 2 9 2   4) 0.0 2 9 2

2. 3) 5.6 1   8) 0.0 2 1 6   7) 0.2 3 1   4) 4.6 4   6) 2 5.2

3. 7) 2 4.5   8) 0.3 3 6   6) 0.0 1 6 2   4) 2 4.4   3) 1.6 8

Problem Solving

Solve each problem.

1. A wire 0.8 inch long is to be cut into 4 pieces each the same length. How long will each piece be?

    Each piece will be _____ inch long.

2. The same amount of flour was used in each of 3 batches of bread dough. A total of 6.9 kilograms was used. How much flour was in each batch?

    _____ kilograms of flour was in each batch.

3. The combined thickness of 5 sheets of metal is 0.015 inch. Each sheet has the same thickness. How thick is each sheet?

    Each sheet is _____ inch thick.

4. Each of 7 bolts has the same weight. Their total weight is 0.42 pound. How much does each bolt weigh?

    Each bolt weighs _____ pound.

5. A machine can make 8 bolts in 0.008 hour. Each bolt takes the same amount of time. How long does it take to make 1 bolt?

    It takes _____ hour to make 1 bolt.

6. Another machine takes 72.4 minutes to make 4 units. Each unit takes the same amount of time. How long does it take to make 1 unit?

    It takes _____ minutes to make 1 unit.

7. A sheet of film is 0.072 centimeter thick. It is 6 times thicker than needed. What thickness is needed?

    _____ centimeter is needed.

8. A sheet of film is 0.0672 inch thick. It is 8 times thicker than needed. What thickness is needed?

    _____ inch is needed.

1.	2.
3.	**4.**
5.	**6.**
7.	**8.**

NAME _____

Lesson 2 Division

Multiply the divisor and the dividend by 10, by 100, or by 1000 so the new divisor is a whole number.

$$0.8)\overline{32} \rightarrow 0.8)\overline{32.0} \rightarrow 8)\overline{320}$$

Multiply by 10.

$$\begin{array}{r} 40 \\ 8)\overline{320} \\ 320 \\ \hline 0 \end{array}$$

$$0.05)\overline{45} \rightarrow 0.05)\overline{45.00} \rightarrow 5)\overline{4500}$$

Multiply by 100.

$$\begin{array}{r} 900 \\ 5)\overline{4500} \\ 4500 \\ \hline 0 \end{array}$$

$$0.004)\overline{26} \rightarrow 0.004)\overline{26.000} \rightarrow 4)\overline{26000}$$

Multiply by 1000.

$$\begin{array}{r} 6,500 \\ 4)\overline{26000} \\ 24000 \\ \hline 2000 \\ 2000 \\ \hline 0 \end{array}$$

Divide.

	a	b	c	d
1.	$0.4)\overline{7\,2}$	$0.3)\overline{8\,1}$	$0.7)\overline{3\,5\,7}$	$0.3)\overline{1\,1\,1}$
2.	$0.03)\overline{5\,4}$	$0.04)\overline{9\,6}$	$0.05)\overline{8\,5}$	$0.08)\overline{2\,9\,6}$
3.	$0.002)\overline{6}$	$0.004)\overline{1\,2}$	$0.006)\overline{2\,4}$	$0.005)\overline{1\,5\,5}$

95

Problem Solving

Solve each problem.

1. Rick put 72 kilograms of honey into jars. He put 0.4 kilogram into each jar. How many jars did he use?

   He used _____ jars.

2. A machine uses 0.3 gallon of fuel each hour. How many hours could the machine operate with 39 gallons of fuel?

   The machine could operate _____ hours.

3. Each metal bar weighs 0.04 kilogram. How many metal bars would weigh 520 kilograms?

   _____ metal bars would weigh 520 kilograms.

4. A machine uses 0.3 gallon of fuel each hour. At that rate, how many hours could the machine operate by using 195 gallons of fuel?

   The machine could operate _____ hours.

5. Eight-tenths gram of a chemical is put into each jar. How many jars can be filled with 192 grams of the chemical?

   _____ jars can be filled.

6. Each sheet of foil is 0.004 inch thick. How many sheets would be in a stack of foil that is 5 inches high?

   There would be _____ sheets.

7. How many nickels ($0.05) are in $6?

   There are _____ nickels in $6.

8. How many nickels are in $10?

   There are _____ nickels in $10.

9. How many nickels are in $16?

   There are _____ nickels in $16.

1.	2.
3.	**4.**
5.	**6.**
7.	**8.**
9.	

Lesson 3 Division

$$0.5\overline{)11.5} \longrightarrow 0.5\overline{)11.5} \longrightarrow 5\overline{)115}$$

Multiply
by 10.

```
  23
5)115
  100
   15
   15
    0
```

$$0.06\overline{)0.426} \longrightarrow 0.06\overline{)0.426} \longrightarrow 6\overline{)42.6}$$

Multiply
by 100.

```
   7.1
6)42.6
  420
    6
    6
    0
```

$$0.003\overline{)2.1} \longrightarrow 0.003\overline{)2.100} \longrightarrow 3\overline{)2100}$$

Multiply
by 1,000.

```
   700
3)2100
  2100
     0
```

Divide.

	a	*b*	*c*	*d*
1.	0.4)7.2	0.3)0.8 1	0.8)0.3 9 2	0.6)5 5.2
2.	0.06)0.8 4	0.04)0.0 6 8	0.08)0.2 2 4	0.07)2.5 2
3.	0.002)0.0 0 8	0.007)0.0 0 4 2	0.008)0.1 4 4	0.009)0.0 3 3 3
4.	0.004)0.0 9 6	0.09)6.3	0.006)0.0 0 9	0.7)8.4

Lesson 4 Division

Divide.

	a	*b*	*c*	*d*

1. $0.03\overline{)1.8}$ $0.06\overline{)2\,8.8}$ $0.04\overline{)9.2}$ $0.05\overline{)1.5}$

2. $0.003\overline{)2.4}$ $0.009\overline{)0.4\,5}$ $0.008\overline{)2.1\,6}$ $0.005\overline{)2.5}$

3. $0.02\overline{)7.4}$ $0.006\overline{)1\,0.2}$ $0.08\overline{)2\,7.2}$ $0.008\overline{)9.6}$

4. $0.05\overline{)3.2\,5}$ $0.06\overline{)4.2}$ $0.002\overline{)0.4}$ $0.004\overline{)0.5\,6}$

5. $0.3\overline{)7\,5}$ $0.007\overline{)5\,6.7}$ $0.09\overline{)7\,4.7}$ $0.005\overline{)4\,8}$

Lesson 5   Division

$$0.08\overline{)0.216} \rightarrow 0.08\overline{)0.216}$$

```
         2.7
0.08) 0.216
      160
       56
       56
        0
```

Check

```
   2.7
 ×0.08
 0.216
```

These should - - - - → 0.216
be the same.

Divide. Check each answer.

	a	b	c

1. $3\overline{)1.44}$ $6\overline{)17.4}$ $5\overline{)0.085}$

2. $0.3\overline{)45}$ $0.003\overline{)12}$ $0.07\overline{)14}$

3. $0.7\overline{)0.98}$ $0.006\overline{)31.8}$ $0.08\overline{)0.632}$

4. $0.03\overline{)4.2}$ $0.004\overline{)7.2}$ $0.006\overline{)1.68}$

5. $0.08\overline{)9.6}$ $0.003\overline{)84}$ $6\overline{)9.6}$

Problem Solving

Solve each problem. Check each answer.

1. Three-tenths pound of chemical is put into each container. How many containers can be filled with 5.4 pounds of chemical?

   _____ containers can be filled.

2. Seventy-five hundredths pound of product Y is to be put into containers that hold 0.5 pound each. How many full containers will there be? What part of the next container will be filled?

   There will be _____ full container.

   _____ of the next container will be filled.

3. There are 10.2 pounds of ball bearings in a box. Each bearing weighs 0.006 pound. How many bearings are in the box?

   There are _____ bearings in the box.

4. A machine processes 1.95 pounds of chemical every 3 hours. At that rate, how many pounds of chemical are processed in 1 hour?

   _____ pounds are processed.

5. Each sheet of metal is 0.005 inch thick. How many sheets of metal would there be in a stack that is 4.2 inches high?

   There would be _____ sheets.

6. A wire that is 0.6 meter long is cut into pieces of the same length. Each piece is 0.06 meter long. How many pieces of wire are there?

   There are _____ pieces.

7. Suppose in problem 6 each piece of wire is 0.006 meter long. How many pieces are there?

   There are _____ pieces.

1.	2.
3.	4.
5.	6.
7.	

Lesson 6   Division

$$0.25\overline{)1} \longrightarrow 0.25\overline{)100} \longrightarrow \begin{array}{r} 4 \\ 25\overline{)100} \\ \underline{100} \\ 0 \end{array}$$

$$2.7\overline{)3.78} \longrightarrow 2.7\overline{)3.78} \longrightarrow \begin{array}{r} 1.4 \\ 27\overline{)37.8} \\ \underline{270} \\ 108 \\ \underline{108} \\ 0 \end{array}$$

Divide.

	a	b	c	d
1.	$0.20\overline{)1}$	$0.15\overline{)9}$	$0.028\overline{)1\,4}$	$0.012\overline{)6}$
2.	$1.2\overline{)3.9\,6}$	$0.42\overline{)0.7\,5\,6}$	$0.18\overline{)0.8\,2\,8}$	$2.5\overline{)0.6\,2\,5}$
3.	$0.67\overline{)0.3\,8\,8\,6}$	$0.45\overline{)1.2\,1\,5}$	$7.3\overline{)3\,0.6\,6}$	$4.3\overline{)0.1\,3\,7\,6}$
4.	$0.025\overline{)7\,5}^{\;3,000}$	$0.36\overline{)1.5\,1\,2}^{\;4.2}$	$5.4\overline{)0.3\,9\,4\,2}^{\;0.073}$	$0.53\overline{)0.6\,3\,6}^{\;1.2}$

Problem Solving

Solve each problem.

1. A carton of items weighs 28.8 pounds. Each item weighs 3.6 pounds. How many items are in the carton?

   _____ items are in the carton.

2. There is 0.444 pound of chemical to be put into tubes. Each tube holds 0.12 pound. How many tubes will be completely filled? How much of another tube will be filled?

   _____ tubes will be filled.

   _____ of the next tube will be filled.

3. A stack of cardboard is 52 inches high. Each piece is 0.65 inch thick. How many pieces of cardboard are in the stack?

   _____ pieces are in the stack.

4. How many pieces each 0.25 inch long can be cut from a wire that is 2 inches long?

   _____ pieces can be cut from the wire.

5. How many pieces each 0.5 inch long can be cut from the wire described in problem 4?

   _____ pieces can be cut from the wire.

6. Each bag of flour weighs 2.2 pounds. How many such bags can be filled by using 11 pounds of flour?

   _____ bags can be filled.

7. Consider the numbers named by 0.016; 1.6; and 0.16. What is the quotient if you divide the greatest number by the least number?

   The quotient is _____.

8. Suppose in problem 7 you divide the least number by the greatest number. What is the quotient?

   The quotient is _____.

1.	2.
3.	**4.**
5.	**6.**
7.	**8.**

102

Lesson 7   Division

$$
\begin{array}{r}
17.2 \\
0.23\overline{)\ 3.956} \\
\underline{2300} \\
1656 \\
\underline{1610} \\
46 \\
\underline{46} \\
0
\end{array}
$$

These should
be the same.

$$
\begin{array}{r}
\textit{Check}\quad 17.2 \\
\times 0.23 \\
\hline
516 \\
\underline{3440} \\
3.956
\end{array}
$$

Divide. Check each answer.

a	*b*	*c*

1. $0.73\overline{)\ 5.9\ 8\ 6}$ $5.6\overline{)\ 0.6\ 7\ 2}$ $0.15\overline{)\ 7\ 5}$

2. $2.1\overline{)\ 6.9\ 3}$ $0.15\overline{)\ 1\ 8}$ $0.083\overline{)\ 6.3\ 0\ 8}$

3. $0.37\overline{)\ 0.1\ 7\ 3\ 9}$ $1.6\overline{)\ 4.4\ 8}$ $0.53\overline{)\ 4.8\ 7\ 6}$

Problem Solving

Solve each problem.

1. A 10-ounce can of fruit costs $0.59. Find the cost per ounce.

   The cost per ounce is $ _____.

2. A 4.75-ounce bar of hand soap costs $0.57. Find the cost per ounce.

   The cost per ounce is $ _____.

3. A 6.5-ounce can of tuna costs $0.91. Find the cost per ounce.

   The cost per ounce is $ _____.

4. A 6.4-ounce tube of toothpaste costs $2.24. Find the cost per ounce.

   The cost per ounce is $ _____.

5. A 147-ounce box of detergent costs $5.88. Find the cost per ounce.

   The cost per ounce is $ _____.

6. Each fish stick weighs 0.8 ounce. One fish stick costs $0.08. Find the cost per ounce.

   The cost per ounce is $ _____.

7. Each slice of cheese weighs 0.75 ounce. There are 20 slices of cheese in a package. The package costs $2.40. Find the cost per ounce.

   The cost per ounce is $ _____.

1.	2.
3.	4.
5.	6.
7.	

CHAPTER 8 TEST

Divide.

	a	*b*	*c*	*d*

1. 8)̄0.1 8 4   3)̄0.4 2   4)̄1 4.8   6)̄0.0 3 0 6

2. 0.05)̄5 5   0.003)̄3 6   0.7)̄4 2   0.04)̄8 4

3. 0.4)̄9.2   0.6)̄0.8 4   0.03)̄0.0 7 2   0.004)̄0.0 2 8

4. 0.006)̄5.4   0.07)̄4.9   0.007)̄0.6 3   0.004)̄4 1.2

5. 0.36)̄9   3.8)̄5.3 2   0.42)̄1.0 9 2   4.5)̄0.3 2 8 5

PRE-TEST—Metric Measurement

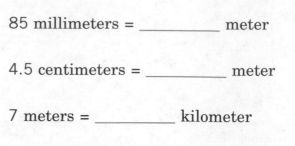

	a	*b*
1.	7 meters = _____ millimeters	85 millimeters = _____ meter
2.	1.9 meters = _____ centimeters	4.5 centimeters = _____ meter
3.	6 kilometers = _____ meters	7 meters = _____ kilometer
4.	5 liters = _____ milliliters	4000 milliliters = _____ liters
5.	3.5 kiloliters = _____ liters	6.5 liters = _____ kiloliter
6.	8.2 kilograms = _____ grams	255 grams = _____ kilogram

Find the area of each rectangle.

a

b

7.

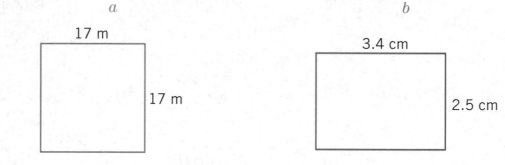

_____ square meters

_____ square centimeters

Find the volume of each rectangular solid.

a

b

8.

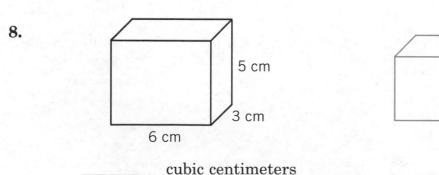

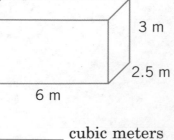

_____ cubic centimeters

_____ cubic meters

Lesson 1 Length

1 millimeter (mm)

1 centimeter (cm)

40 mm or 4 cm

10 mm = 1 cm		1 mm = 0.1 cm
1000 mm = 1 m		1 mm = 0.001 m
100 cm = 1 m		1 cm = 0.01 m
1000 m = 1 km		1 m = 0.001 km

CENTIMETERS 2 3 4 5 6

100 cm or 1 meter (m)

CENTIMETERS 2 3 4 5 6 7   95 96 97 98 99 100

A distance of 1000 meters is 1 kilometer (km).

Measure the following to the nearest meter.

a   *b*

1. height of classroom door _____ m   width of room _____ m

2. width of classroom door _____ m   length of room _____ m

3. One kilometer is about the length of 5 blocks.
   About how many kilometers do you live from school? _____ km

Find the length of each line segment to the nearest centimeter.

4. _____ cm

5. _____ cm

Find the length of each line segment to the nearest millimeter.

6. _____ mm

7. _____ mm

Draw a line segment for each measurement.

8. 6 cm

9. 8 cm

10. 35 mm

NAME _____

Lesson 2 Units of Length

160 m = _____?_____ km   7.2 cm = _____?_____ mm

1 m = 0.001 km   1 cm = 10 mm
(160 × 1) m = (160 × 0.001) km   (7.2 × 1) cm = (7.2 × 10) mm

160 m = ___0.16___ km   7.2 cm = ___72___ mm

Find the length of each line segment to the nearest millimeter.
Then give the length in centimeters and in meters.

	a	b	c

1. _____ mm _____ cm _____ m

2. _____ mm _____ cm _____ m

3. _____ mm _____ cm _____ m

4. _____ mm _____ cm _____ m

5. _____ mm _____ cm _____ m

Complete the following.

a   b   c

6. 54 mm = _____ cm   8 m = _____ mm   234 m = _____ km

7. 1.6 m = _____ cm   0.9 cm = _____ mm   58 mm = _____ cm

8. 612 mm = _____ m   4 km = _____ m   13 mm = _____ cm

9. 0.02 m = _____ mm   0.75 km = _____ m   34.5 m = _____ km

10. 707 cm = _____ m   0.005 m = _____ cm   465 mm = _____ cm

108

Lesson 3 Area PRE-ALGEBRA

To find the *area measure (A)* of a rectangle, multiply the measure of its *length (l)* by the measure of its *width (w).*

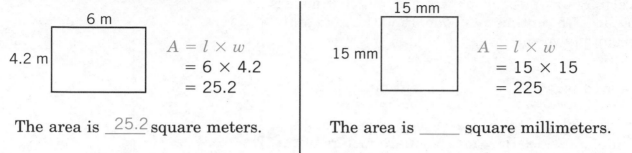

6 m

4.2 m

$A = l \times w$
$= 6 \times 4.2$
$= 25.2$

The area is __25.2__ square meters.

15 mm

15 mm

$A = l \times w$
$= 15 \times 15$
$= 225$

The area is _____ square millimeters.

Measure the sides as indicated. Then find the area of each rectangle.

a   *b*

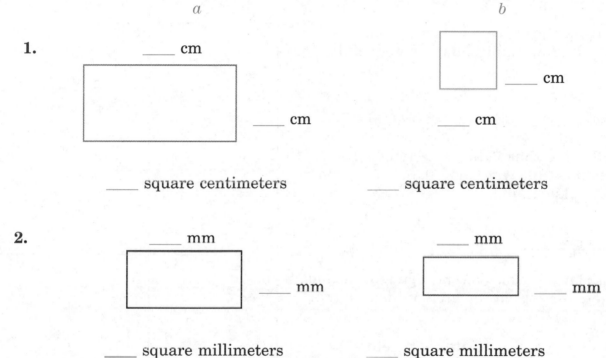

1. _____ cm

_____ cm

_____ square centimeters

_____ cm

_____ cm

_____ square centimeters

2. _____ mm

_____ mm

_____ square millimeters

_____ mm

_____ mm

_____ square millimeters

Find the area of each rectangle described below.

	length	width	area
3.	5.8 km	3 km	_____ square kilometers
4.	4.5 m	4.5 m	_____ square meters
5.	32.4 m	16 m	_____ square meters

Problem Solving   PRE-ALGEBRA

Solve each problem.

1. A rectangular piece of plywood is 150 centimeters long. It is 75 centimeters wide. Find the area of the piece of plywood.

   The area is _____ square centimeters.

2. A rectangular piece of carpet is 6 meters long and 4.5 meters wide. How many square meters of carpet is that?

   That is _____ square meters of carpet.

3. A rectangular floor is 8.5 meters long and 6.5 meters wide. How many square meters of floor are there?

   There are _____ square meters of floor.

4. A playground is shaped like a rectangle. Its length is 140 meters. Its width is 60 meters. Find the area of the playground.

   The area is _____ square meters.

5. A rectangular poster is 35 centimeters wide and 52 centimeters long. Find the area of the poster.

   The area is _____ square centimeters.

6. A rectangular postcard is 8.5 centimeters wide and 14 centimeters long. Find the area of the postcard.

   The area is _____ square centimeters.

7. A rectangular field is 1000 meters long and 800 meters wide. How many square meters are in that field?

   There are _____ square meters in the field.

1.	2.
3.	4.
5.	6.
7.	

Lesson 4 Volume   PRE-ALGEBRA

To determine the *volume measure (V)* of a rectangular solid, find the product of the measure of its *length (l)*, the measure of its *width (w)*, and the measure of its *height (h)*.

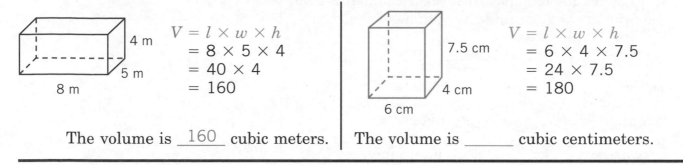

$V = l \times w \times h$
$= 8 \times 5 \times 4$
$= 40 \times 4$
$= 160$

$V = l \times w \times h$
$= 6 \times 4 \times 7.5$
$= 24 \times 7.5$
$= 180$

The volume is __160__ cubic meters. │ The volume is _____ cubic centimeters.

Find the volume of each rectangular solid below.

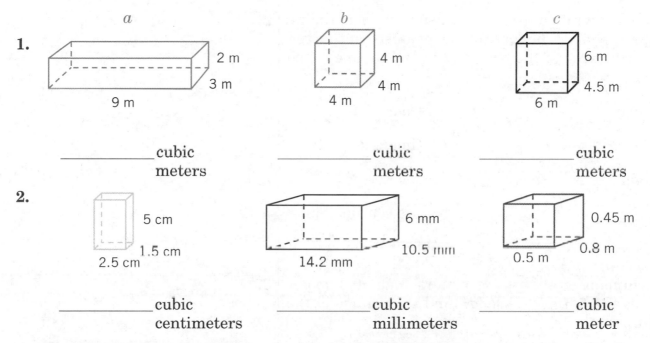

	a	*b*	*c*

1.   2 m, 3 m, 9 m   4 m, 4 m, 4 m   6 m, 4.5 m, 6 m

_____ cubic meters   _____ cubic meters   _____ cubic meters

2.   5 cm, 1.5 cm, 2.5 cm   6 mm, 10.5 mm, 14.2 mm   0.45 m, 0.8 m, 0.5 m

_____ cubic centimeters   _____ cubic millimeters   _____ cubic meter

Find the volume of each rectangular solid described below.

	length	width	height	volume
3.	7 m	6 m	5 m	_____ cubic meters
4.	9.2 cm	4.5 cm	3 cm	_____ cubic centimeters
5.	8.5 mm	8.5 mm	8.5 mm	_____ cubic millimeters
6.	7.2 cm	6.2 cm	5.2 cm	_____ cubic centimeters

Problem Solving   PRE-ALGEBRA

Solve each problem.

1. Find a rectangular room. Measure its length, its width, and its height to the nearest meter. Find the area of the floor and the volume of the room.

   length: _____ meters

   width: _____ meters

   height: _____ meters

   floor area: _____ square meters

   volume: _____ cubic meters

   1.

2. Find a rectangular box. Measure its length, its width, and its height to the nearest centimeter. Find the area of the box top and the volume of the box.

   length: _____ centimeters

   width: _____ centimeters

   height: _____ centimeters

   top area: _____ square centimeters

   volume: _____ cubic centimeters

   2.

3. A shipping crate is 1.2 meters high, 0.8 meter wide, and 2.5 meters long. Find the volume of the crate.

   The volume is _____ cubic meters.

   3.

4. A book is 28 centimeters long, 21 centimeters wide, and 1 centimeter thick. How much space does the book occupy?

   It occupies _____ cubic centimeters of space.

   4.

5. A hole was dug 12.5 meters long, 10.5 meters wide, and 2 meters deep. How many cubic meters of dirt were removed?

   _____ cubic meters of dirt were removed.

   5.

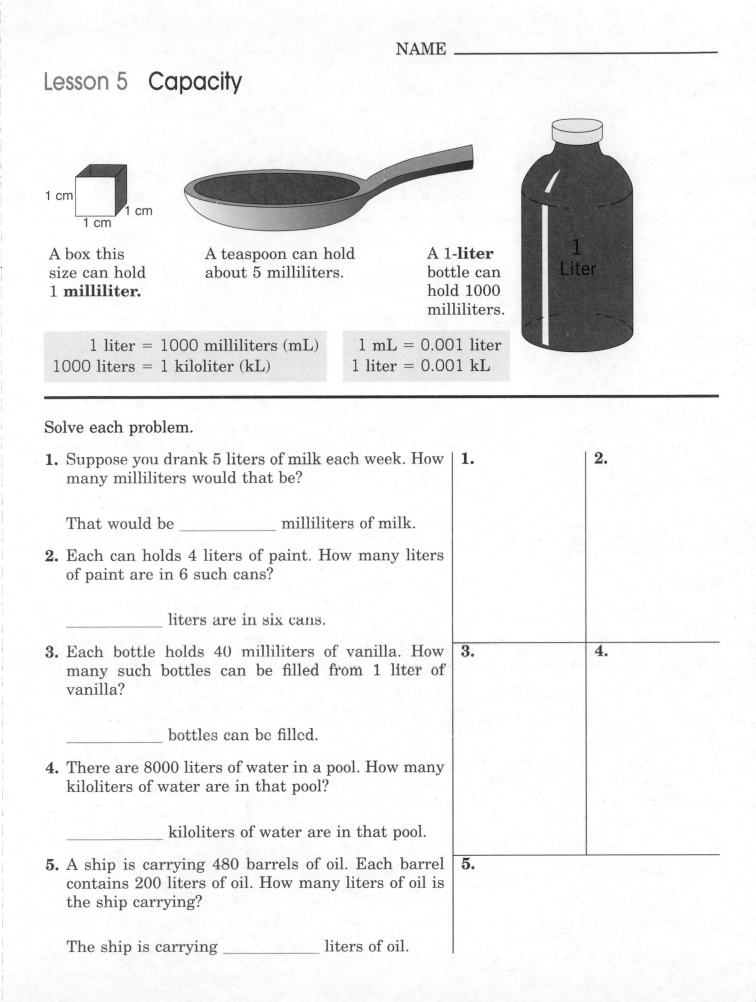

Lesson 5   Capacity

1 cm 1 cm 1 cm

A box this size can hold **1 milliliter.**

A teaspoon can hold about 5 milliliters.

A 1-**liter** bottle can hold 1000 milliliters.

1 Liter

| 1 liter = 1000 milliliters (mL) | 1 mL = 0.001 liter |
| 1000 liters = 1 kiloliter (kL) | 1 liter = 0.001 kL |

Solve each problem.

1. Suppose you drank 5 liters of milk each week. How many milliliters would that be?

That would be _____ milliliters of milk.

2. Each can holds 4 liters of paint. How many liters of paint are in 6 such cans?

_____ liters are in six cans.

3. Each bottle holds 40 milliliters of vanilla. How many such bottles can be filled from 1 liter of vanilla?

_____ bottles can be filled.

4. There are 8000 liters of water in a pool. How many kiloliters of water are in that pool?

_____ kiloliters of water are in that pool.

5. A ship is carrying 480 barrels of oil. Each barrel contains 200 liters of oil. How many liters of oil is the ship carrying?

The ship is carrying _____ liters of oil.

1.

2.

3.

4.

5.

Lesson 6   Units of Capacity

65 liters = _____?_____ mL   5.2 liters = _____?_____ kL

1 liter = 1000 mL   1 liter = 0.001 kL
(65 × 1) liters = (65 × 1000) mL   (5.2 × 1) liters = (5.2 × 0.001) kL

65 liters = ___65,000___ mL   5.2 liters = ___0.0052___ kL

Complete the following.

  a   b

1.   7 liters = _____ mL   0.5 liter = _____ mL

2.   5 mL = _____ liter   4500 mL = _____ liters

3.   7.5 kL = _____ liters   2.54 kL = _____ liters

4.   600 liters = _____ kL   7.5 liters = _____ kL

5.   3.4 liters = _____ mL   300 mL = _____ liter

6.   3 kL = _____ liters   300 liters = _____ kL

7.   0.6 liter = _____ kL   24 kL = _____ liters

8.   47 mL = _____ liter   0.75 liter = _____ mL

Solve.

9.   Consider filling the tank shown with water. How
many milliliters would the tank hold? How many
liters? (Hint: A 1-cubic-centimeter container can hold
1 milliliter of water.)

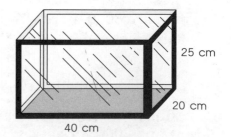

25 cm
20 cm
40 cm

The tank would hold _____ milliliters.

The tank would hold _____ liters.

Lesson 7 Weight

2 paper clips weigh
about 1 **gram** (g).

1 nickel weighs
about 5 grams.

200 nickels weigh about
1000 grams or 1 **kilogram** (kg).

1 g = 1000 milligrams (mg)	1 mg = 0.001 g
1 kg = 1000 g	1 g = 0.001 kg

Solve each problem.

1. There are 100 paper clips in a box. How many grams would a box of paper clips weigh?

   It would weigh _____ grams.

2. There are 20 boxes of paper clips in a carton. How many grams would a carton of paper clips weigh?

   The carton would weigh _____ grams.

3. How many grams would a roll of 40 nickels weigh?

   The roll would weigh _____ grams.

4. How many nickels would weigh 5 kilograms?

   _____ nickels would weigh 5 kilograms.

5. A truck is hauling 6 crates. Each crate weighs 35 kilograms. How much do all the crates weigh?

   They weigh _____ kilograms.

1.

2.

3.

4.

5.

Lesson 8   Units of Weight

73 kg = _____?_____ g

1 kg = 1000 g
(73 × 1) kg = (73 × 1000) g

73 kg = __73,000__ g

54 mg = _____?_____ g

1 mg = 0.001 g
(54 × 1) mg = (54 × 0.001) g

54 mg = __0.054__ g

Complete the following.

	a	*b*
1.	8 kg = _____ g	7.5 kg = _____ g
2.	4500 mg = _____ g	38 g = _____ kg
3.	6 g = _____ mg	640 mg = _____ g
4.	0.05 kg = _____ g	4.5 kg = _____ g
5.	0.007 kg = _____ g	7000 g = _____ kg
6.	5.5 g = _____ mg	0.21 g = _____ mg
7.	0.4 kg = _____ g	345 g = _____ kg
8.	607 mg = _____ g	8.9 g = _____ mg
9.	52 g = _____ mg	975 g = _____ kg

Solve.

10. Consider this tank filled with water. Assume that 1 liter of water weighs 1 kilogram. How many kilograms would the water in the tank weigh?

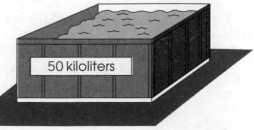

50 kiloliters

The water would weigh _____ kilograms.

CHAPTER 9 TEST

Complete the following.

	a	b
1.	9 m = _____ mm	365 mm = _____ m
2.	7.2 m = _____ cm	8.4 cm = _____ m
3.	26 km = _____ m	17 m = _____ km
4.	4.51 liters = _____ mL	65 mL = _____ liter
5.	6.8 kL = _____ liters	3500 liters = _____ kL
6.	0.9 kg = _____ g	785 g = _____ kg
7.	2 g = _____ mg	0.998 kg = _____ g
8.	1500 m = _____ km	0.45 kg = _____ g

Find the area of each rectangle.

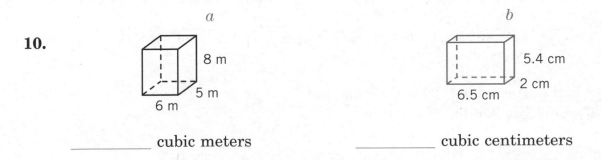

                    a b

9.   4.5 cm   2.8 km

         5.6 cm   3.5 km

_____ square centimeters   _____ square kilometers

Find the volume of each rectangular solid.

                    a b

10.   8 m   5.4 cm

           5 m   2 cm

       6 m   6.5 cm

_____ cubic meters   _____ cubic centimeters

PRE-TEST—Measurement

Complete the following.

	a		*b*

1. 3 feet = _____ inches   48 inches = _____ feet

2. 6 yards = _____ feet   24 feet = _____ yards

3. 2 miles = _____ feet   3 miles = _____ yards

4. 3 pints = _____ cups   14 cups = _____ pints

5. 7 quarts = _____ pints   8 quarts = _____ gallons

6. 2 pounds = _____ ounces   2,000 pounds = _____ ton

7. 6 minutes = _____ seconds   180 seconds = _____ minutes

8. 48 hours = _____ days   120 minutes = _____ hours

9. 4 feet 8 inches = _____ inches

10. 3 gallons 3 quarts = _____ quarts

11. 2 pounds 6 ounces = _____ ounces

12. 2 minutes 30 seconds = _____ seconds

Find the area of each figure.

	a		*b*

13.

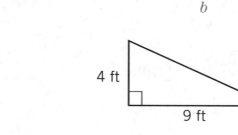

_____ square inches

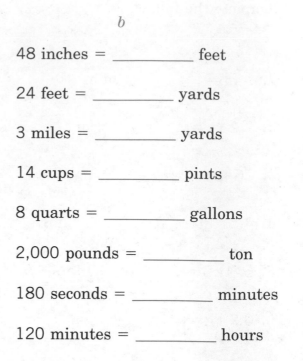

_____ square feet

Solve.

14. A shoe box is 6 inches wide, 11 inches long, and 5 inches high. Find the volume of the box.

The volume is _____ cubic inches.

NAME _____

Lesson 1   Length

| 1 foot (ft) = 12 inches (in.) |
| 1 yard (yd) = 3 ft |
| 1 yd = 36 in. |
| 1 mile (mi) = 5,280 ft |

| $1 \text{ in.} = \frac{1}{12} \text{ ft}$ |
| $1 \text{ ft} = \frac{1}{3} \text{ yd}$ |
| $1 \text{ in.} = \frac{1}{36} \text{ yd}$ |
| 1 mi = 1,760 yd |

36 in. = ____?____ ft

$1 \text{ in.} = \frac{1}{12} \text{ ft}$

$(36 \times 1) \text{ in.} = (36 \times \frac{1}{12}) \text{ ft}$

36 in. = ___3___ ft

6 ft 4 in. = ____?____ in.

1 ft = 12 in.

6 ft = (6 × 12) or 72 in.

6 ft 4 in. = (72 + 4) in.

6 ft 4 in. = ___76___ in.

Complete the following.

a *b*

1. 6 ft = _____ in.   60 in. = _____ ft

2. 9 yd = _____ ft   12 ft = _____ yd

3. 5 yd = _____ in.   144 in. = _____ yd

4. 3 mi = _____ ft   3 mi = _____ yd

5. 5 yd = _____ ft   18 in. = _____ ft

6. 2 mi = _____ ft   5 mi = _____ yd

7. 5 ft 4 in. = _____ in.

8. 3 yd 5 in. = _____ in.

9. 5 yd 2 ft = _____ ft

10. 9 ft 6 in. = _____ in.

11. 1 mi 750 ft = _____ ft

Problem Solving

Solve each problem.

1. The top of a doorway is 84 inches above the floor. What is the height of the doorway in feet?

   The doorway is _____ feet high.

2. The distance along the foul line from home plate to the right field fence is 336 feet. What is this distance in yards?

   This distance is _____ yards.

3. A kite string is 125 yards long. How many feet long is the string?

   The string is _____ feet long.

4. A snake is 4 feet 3 inches long. What is the length of the snake in inches?

   Its length is _____ inches.

5. A rope is 5 feet 9 inches long. What is the length of the rope in inches?

   The rope is _____ inches long.

6. The distance across a street is 15 yards 1 foot. What is this distance in feet?

   This distance is _____ feet.

7. A doorway is 2 feet 8 inches wide. What is the width of the doorway in inches?

   The doorway is _____ inches wide.

8. Laura is 4 feet 11 inches tall. What is her height in inches?

   Laura is _____ inches tall.

9. Aaron is 5 feet 4 inches tall. What is his height in inches?

   Aaron is _____ inches tall.

1.	2.
3.	4.
5.	6.
7.	8.
9.	

Lesson 2 Area   PRE-ALGEBRA

To determine the *area measure* (A) of a right triangle, find *one-half* the product of the measure of its *base* (b) and the measure of its *height* (h).

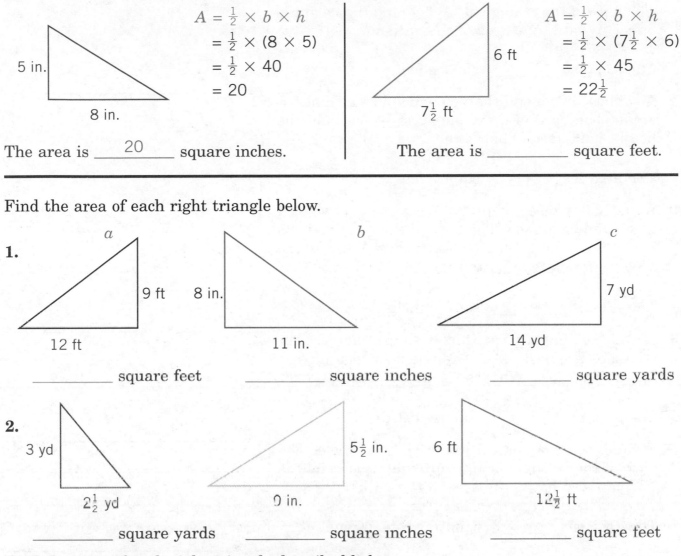

$A = \frac{1}{2} \times b \times h$
$= \frac{1}{2} \times (8 \times 5)$
$= \frac{1}{2} \times 40$
$= 20$

The area is ____20____ square inches.

$A = \frac{1}{2} \times b \times h$
$= \frac{1}{2} \times (7\frac{1}{2} \times 6)$
$= \frac{1}{2} \times 45$
$= 22\frac{1}{2}$

The area is _____ square feet.

Find the area of each right triangle below.

1.

a
9 ft
12 ft
_____ square feet

b
8 in.
11 in.
_____ square inches

c
7 yd
14 yd
_____ square yards

2.

3 yd
$2\frac{1}{2}$ yd
_____ square yards

$5\frac{1}{2}$ in.
9 in.
_____ square inches

6 ft
$12\frac{1}{2}$ ft
_____ square feet

Find the area of each right triangle described below.

	base	height	area
3.	8 ft	9 ft	_____ square feet
4.	7 yd	5 yd	_____ square yards
5.	$4\frac{1}{2}$ in.	6 in.	_____ square inches
6.	5 ft	$3\frac{1}{2}$ ft	_____ square feet
7.	$3\frac{3}{4}$ in.	2 in.	_____ square inches

Problem Solving   PRE-ALGEBRA

Solve each problem.

1. The edges of a flower garden form a right triangle. The base of the triangle is 16 feet and the height is 8 feet. What is the area of the garden?

   The area is _____ square feet.

1. _____

2. A sailboat has a sail that is shaped like a right triangle. The base of the triangle is 14 feet and the height is 20 feet. What is the area of the sail?

   The area is _____ square feet.

2. _____

3. Anne has a piece of poster board that is shaped like a right triangle. The base of the triangle is 28 inches and the height is $16\frac{1}{2}$ inches. What is the area of the piece of poster board?

   The area is _____ square inches.

3. _____

4. Mr. McKee has a patio that is shaped like a right triangle. The base of the triangle is 36 feet and the height is 12 feet. What is the area of the patio?

   The area is _____ square feet.

4. _____

5. A small park is shaped like a right triangle. The base of the triangle is 160 yards and the height is 120 yards. What is the area of the park?

   The area is _____ square yards.

5. _____

6. Nelson has a piece of sheet metal that is shaped like a right triangle. The base of the triangle is 16 inches and the height is $12\frac{1}{2}$ inches. What is the area of the piece of sheet metal?

   The area is _____ square inches.

6. _____

7. Mrs. Jones has a piece of material that is shaped like a right triangle. The base of the triangle is $25\frac{1}{2}$ inches and the height is 18 inches. What is the area of the piece of material?

   The area is _____ square inches.

7. _____

Lesson 3   Area and Volume   PRE-ALGEBRA

Find the area of each right triangle or rectangle below.

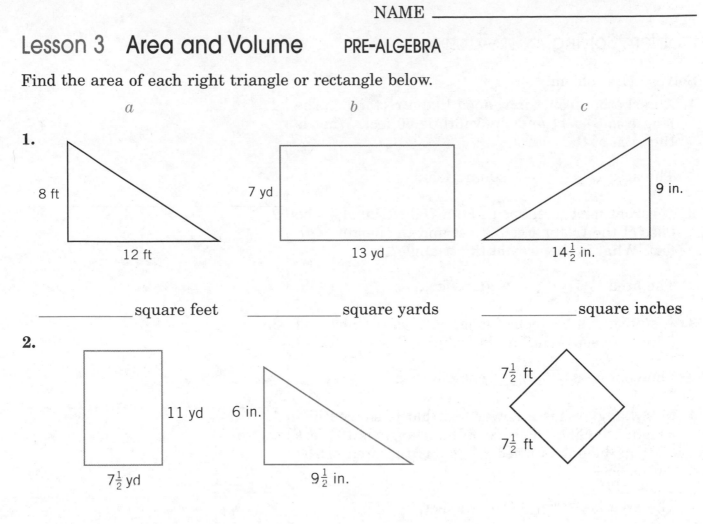

	a	b	c
1.	8 ft / 12 ft	7 yd / 13 yd	9 in. / 14½ in.
	_____ square feet	_____ square yards	_____ square inches

2.

11 yd / 7½ yd   6 in. / 9½ in.   7½ ft / 7½ ft

_____ square yards   _____ square inches   _____ square feet

Find the volume of each rectangular solid described below.

	length	width	height	volume
3.	7 yd	5 yd	3 yd	_____ cubic yards
4.	9 in.	5 in.	4½ in.	_____ cubic inches
5.	6 ft	3¼ ft	9 ft	_____ cubic feet
6.	5½ yd	3 yd	7 yd	_____ cubic yards
7.	3¼ in.	2¾ in.	4 in.	_____ cubic inches
8.	6½ ft	5 ft	4½ ft	_____ cubic feet
9.	3 in.	5¼ in.	3½ in.	_____ cubic inches
10.	9¼ ft	8¾ ft	5 ft	_____ cubic feet

Problem Solving   PRE-ALGEBRA

Solve each problem.

1. A basketball court is shaped like a rectangle. The length is 84 feet and the width is 50 feet. What is the area of the court?

   The area is _____ square feet.

   1.

2. A garden plot is shaped like a right triangle. The base of the triangle is 50 feet and the height is 18 feet. What is the area of the triangle?

   The area is _____ square feet.

   2.

3. A suitcase is 32 inches long, 16 inches wide, and 6 inches deep. What is the volume of the suitcase?

   The volume is _____ cubic inches.

   3.

4. Mrs. Langley has a flower bed that is shaped like a right triangle. The base of the triangle is $12\frac{1}{2}$ feet and the height is 6 feet. What is the area of the flower bed?

   The area is _____ square feet.

   4.

5. A plot of land is shaped like a rectangle. It is 280 yards long and 90 yards wide. What is the area of the plot?

   The area is _____ square yards.

   5.

6. A box is 9 inches long, $6\frac{1}{2}$ inches wide, and $1\frac{1}{2}$ inches deep. What is the volume of the box?

   The volume is _____ cubic inches.

   6.

7. A rectangular tabletop is 72 inches long and 36 inches wide. What is the area of the tabletop?

   The area is _____ square inches.

   7.

8. A brick is 8 inches long, 3 inches wide, and 2 inches high. How much space does the brick occupy?

   The brick occupies _____ cubic inches of space.

   8.

Lesson 4   Capacity

| 1 pint (pt) = 2 cups |
| 1 quart (qt) = 2 pt |
| 1 gallon (gal) = 4 qt |

| 1 cup = $\frac{1}{2}$ pt |
| 1 pt = $\frac{1}{2}$ qt |
| 1 qt = $\frac{1}{4}$ gal |

5 pt = ____?____ qt

1 pt = $\frac{1}{2}$ qt
5 pt = ($\frac{1}{2}$ × 5) qt

5 pt = ____$2\frac{1}{2}$____ qt

3 gal 2 qt = ____?____ qt

1 gal = 4 qt
3 gal = (3 × 4) or 12 qt
3 gal 2 qt = (12 + 2) qt

3 gal 2 qt = ____14____ qt

Complete the following.

a 　　　　　　　　　　　　　　b

1. 3 pt = _____ cups　　　　　8 cups = _____ pt

2. 5 qt = _____ pt　　　　　　10 pt = _____ qt

3. 4 gal = _____ qt　　　　　11 qt = _____ gal

4. 24 qt = _____ gal　　　　15 pt = _____ qt

5. 2 pt 1 cup = _____ cups

6. 5 gal 3 qt = _____ qt

7. 2 qt 1 pt = _____ pt

8. 4 gal 3 qt = _____ qt

9. An aquarium holds 3 gallons 3 quarts of water.
How many quarts would this be? How many pints?
How many cups?

This would be _____ quarts.

This would be _____ pints.

This would be _____ cups.

Lesson 5   Weight and Time

1 pound (lb) = 16 ounces (oz)
1 ton = 2,000 lb

$1 \text{ oz} = \frac{1}{16} \text{ lb}$

1 minute (min) = 60 seconds (sec)
1 hour = 60 min
1 day = 24 hours

$1 \text{ sec} = \frac{1}{60} \text{ min}$
$1 \text{ min} = \frac{1}{60} \text{ hour}$
$1 \text{ hour} = \frac{1}{24} \text{ day}$

80 oz = _____?_____ lb

$1 \text{ oz} = \frac{1}{16} \text{ lb}$
$80 \text{ oz} = (80 \times \frac{1}{16}) \text{ lb}$

80 oz = ____5____ lb

1 min 12 sec = _____?_____ sec

1 min = 60 sec
1 min 12 sec = (60 + 12) sec

1 min 12 sec = ____72____ sec

Complete the following.

	a	*b*
1.	72 lb = _____ oz	80 oz = _____ lb
2.	4 tons = _____ lb	6,000 lb = _____ tons
3.	3 min = _____ sec	120 sec = _____ min
4.	5 hours = _____ min	360 min = _____ hours
5.	5 days = _____ hours	144 hours = _____ days
6.	3 lb 12 oz = _____ oz	5 lb 6 oz = _____ oz
7.	3 tons 500 lb = _____ lb	
8.	2 hr 45 min = _____ min	
9.	4 days 12 hours = _____ hours	
10.	4 hours 20 min = _____ min	
11.	2 days 8 hours = _____ hours	

CHAPTER 10 TEST

Complete the following.

	a	*b*

1. 8 ft = _____ in.   72 in. = _____ ft

2. 5 yd = _____ ft   30 ft = _____ yd

3. 2 mi = _____ ft   1 mi = _____ yd

4. 6 pt = _____ cups   11 cups = _____ pt

5. 18 qt = _____ pt   12 pt = _____ qt

6. 5 gal = _____ qt   4,000 lb = _____ tons

7. 6 lb = _____ oz   32 oz = _____ lb

8. 5 min = _____ sec   120 sec = _____ min

9. 5 ft 10 in. = _____ in.   2 days = _____ hours

10. 4 gal 1 qt = _____ qt   72 hours = _____ days

11. 4 lb 12 oz = _____ oz

12. 3 hours 30 min = _____ min

Solve.

13. A box is 36 inches long, 12 inches wide, and 10 inches high. Find the volume of the box.

The volume of the box is _____ cubic inches.

Find the area of each figure.

	a	*b*

14.

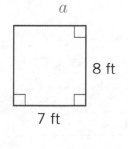

8 ft

7 ft

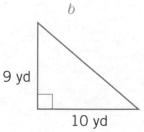

9 yd

10 yd

_____ square feet   _____ square yards

PRE-TEST—Percent

Complete the following.

	a		b

1. $\dfrac{7}{100}$ = _____ % $\dfrac{9}{10}$ = _____ %

2. $\dfrac{7}{20}$ = _____ % $\dfrac{13}{25}$ = _____ %

3. 0.07 = _____ %   0.4 = _____ %

4. 0.135 = _____ %   1.35 = _____ %

Change each percent to a decimal.

       a b

5.   6% = _____   67% = _____

6. 6.25% = _____   125% = _____

Change each percent to a fraction in simplest form.

       a b

7.   9% = _____   20% = _____

8. 45% = _____   56% = _____

Complete the following.

       a b

9.   1% of 59 = _____   10% of 75 = _____

10.   100% of 84 = _____   45% of 89 = _____

11.   75% of 48 = _____   83% of 147 = _____

12.   12% of 180 = _____   7.5% of 840 = _____

13. 6.75% of 500 = _____   8.5% of 96.4 = _____

14. 12.5% of 420 = _____   7% of 79.3 = _____

Lesson 1   Percent

The symbol % (read **percent**) means $\frac{1}{100}$ or 0.01.

$$3\% = 3 \times \frac{1}{100} \text{ or } 3\% = 3 \times 0.01 \qquad 17\% = 17 \times \frac{1}{100} \text{ or } 17\% = 17 \times 0.01$$

$$= \underline{\quad \frac{3}{100} \quad} \qquad = \underline{\quad 0.03 \quad} \qquad = \underline{\qquad\qquad} \qquad = \underline{\qquad\qquad}$$

Complete the following.

	percent	fraction	decimal
1.	1%	_____	_____
2.	7%	_____	_____
3.	29%	_____	_____
4.	47%	_____	_____
5.	53%	_____	_____
6.	21%	_____	_____
7.	83%	_____	_____
8.	49%	_____	_____
9.	61%	_____	_____
10.	9%	_____	_____
11.	37%	_____	_____
12.	77%	_____	_____
13.	91%	_____	_____
14.	33%	_____	_____

Lesson 2 Percent and Fractions

Study how a percent is changed to a fraction or mixed numeral in simplest form.

$$75\% = 75 \times \frac{1}{100}$$

$$= \frac{75}{100}$$

$$= \underline{\frac{3}{4}}$$

$$125\% = 125 \times \frac{1}{100}$$

$$= \frac{125}{100}$$

$$= \frac{5}{4} \text{ or } \underline{\hspace{2cm}}$$

Study how a fraction or mixed numeral is changed to a percent.

$$\frac{1}{2} = \frac{1}{2} \times \frac{50}{50}$$

$$= \frac{50}{100}$$

$$= 50 \times \frac{1}{100}$$

$$= \underline{50}\ \%$$

$$1\frac{3}{4} = \frac{7}{4} \times \frac{25}{25}$$

$$= \frac{175}{100}$$

$$= 175 \times \frac{1}{100}$$

$$= \underline{\hspace{1.5cm}}\%$$

Change each of the following to a fraction or mixed numeral in simplest form.

	a	b	c
1.	25% = _____	45% = _____	160% = _____
2.	65% = _____	120% = _____	24% = _____
3.	78% = _____	55% = _____	260% = _____
4.	70% = _____	144% = _____	86% = _____
5.	95% = _____	40% = _____	180% = _____

Change each of the following to a percent.

	a	b	c
6.	$\frac{1}{5}$ = _____	$\frac{3}{4}$ = _____	$\frac{1}{20}$ = _____
7.	$2\frac{7}{50}$ = _____	$\frac{3}{5}$ = _____	$1\frac{1}{5}$ = _____
8.	$\frac{9}{10}$ = _____	$\frac{7}{25}$ = _____	$2\frac{1}{4}$ = _____
9.	$1\frac{3}{5}$ = _____	$\frac{3}{10}$ = _____	$\frac{4}{25}$ = _____
10.	$\frac{7}{20}$ = _____	$\frac{31}{50}$ = _____	$1\frac{2}{5}$ = _____

Lesson 3 Percent and Decimals

Study how a percent is changed to a decimal.

$12.5\% = 12.5 \times 0.01$ $1.25\% = 1.25 \times 0.01$

$= \underline{\quad 0.125 \quad}$ $= \underline{\qquad}$

Study how a decimal is changed to a percent.

$0.7 = 0.70$ $0.245 = 24.5 \times 0.01$

$\quad = 70 \times 0.01$

$\quad = \underline{\quad 70\% \quad}$ $= \underline{\qquad}\%$

Change each of the following to a decimal.

	a	b	c
1.	$13.5\% = $ _____	$37\% = $ _____	$6.25\% = $ _____
2.	$6.5\% = $ _____	$4.75\% = $ _____	$2.75\% = $ _____
3.	$7\% = $ _____	$62.5\% = $ _____	$8.5\% = $ _____
4.	$32.5\% = $ _____	$8.75\% = $ _____	$9.5\% = $ _____
5.	$8.25\% = $ _____	$17.5\% = $ _____	$3.75\% = $ _____
6.	$0.75\% = $ _____	$7.25\% = $ _____	$1.75\% = $ _____

Change each of the following to a percent.

	a	b	c
7.	$0.6 = $ _____	$0.52 = $ _____	$0.325 = $ _____
8.	$0.2475 = $ _____	$0.8 = $ _____	$0.65 = $ _____
9.	$0.145 = $ _____	$0.1675 = $ _____	$0.5 = $ _____
10.	$0.06 = $ _____	$0.007 = $ _____	$0.0625 = $ _____
11.	$0.075 = $ _____	$0.0075 = $ _____	$0.005 = $ _____
12.	$0.9 = $ _____	$0.19 = $ _____	$0.385 = $ _____

Problem Solving

Solve each problem.

1. Three-fourths of the students in class are girls. What percent of the students are girls?

   _____ of the students are girls.

   1.

2. Mr. Beck received 65% of the votes cast. What fractional part of the votes did he receive?

   He received _____ of the votes.

   2.

3. Marty made a base hit on 25% of his official times at bat. What is his batting average? (Note: Batting averages are usually expressed as thousandths.)

   His average is _____.

   3.

4. Four-fifths of the students are in the gym. What percent of the students are in the gym?

   _____ of the students are in the gym.

   4.

5. A farmer has 45% of a field plowed. Write a fraction to tell how much of the field is plowed.

   _____ of the field is plowed.

   5.

6. The Cubs won 61.5% of their games last year. How can this percent be expressed as a decimal?

   61.5% can be expressed as _____.

   6.

7. A certain player has a fielding average of .987. How can this fielding average be expressed as a percent?

   This average can be expressed as _____.

   7.

8. Seven-tenths of the customers at the Caribbean Market come in the morning. What percent of the customers come in the morning?

   _____ of the customers come in the morning.

   8.

Lesson 4   Percent of a Number

Study how fractions are used to find a percent of a number.

$$75\% \text{ of } 60 = 75\% \times 60$$
$$= \frac{75}{100} \times 60$$
$$= \frac{3}{4} \times \frac{60}{1}$$
$$= \frac{3 \times 60}{4 \times 1}$$
$$= \frac{180}{4} \text{ or } 45$$

$$125\% \text{ of } 37.5 = 125\% \times 37.5$$
$$= \frac{125}{100} \times 37.5$$
$$= \frac{5}{4} \times \frac{375}{10}$$
$$= \frac{5 \times 375}{4 \times 10}$$
$$= \frac{1875}{40} \text{ or } 46\frac{7}{8}$$

75% of 60 = ____45____   125% of 37.5 = _____

Write each answer in simplest form.

a b

1.   6% of 75 = _____   108% of 63.5 = _____

2.   50% of 32 = _____   75% of 12.6 = _____

3.   20% of 68 = _____   25% of 72.8 = _____

4.   5% of 48 = _____   15% of 52.4 = _____

5.   104% of 35 = _____   136% of 7.5 = _____

6.   55% of 5.25 = _____   80% of 160 = _____

7.   166% of 60 = _____   90% of 1.8 = _____

8.   72% of 7.25 = _____   140% of 240 = _____

9.   60% of 9.8 = _____   250% of 90 = _____

10.   100% of 725 = _____   40% of 9.6 = _____

Problem Solving

Solve each problem.

1. Twenty-five percent of the workers are on the third shift. There are 132 workers in all. How many of them are on the third shift?

   _____ are on the third shift.

2. The enrollment at Franklin School has increased 20% from last year. The enrollment last year was 750. By how many students has the enrollment increased?

   Enrollment has increased by _____ students.

3. Ms. Allan is paid 5% of her total sales. How much would she earn in a week if her total sales were $2,800?

   She would earn _____.

4. Forty percent of the class finished their assignment before lunch. There are 25 students in the class. How many students finished before lunch?

   _____ students finished before lunch.

5. The tax on a certain item is 10% of the sales price. What would be the amount of tax on an item that sells for $60?

   The tax would be _____.

6. It is estimated that a new truck will be worth 75% of its original cost after one year. How much would a 1-year-old truck be worth that originally sold for $5,600?

   The truck would be worth _____.

7. Fifty percent of the people questioned in a sales survey indicated a preference for Brand X. There were 7,520 people questioned. How many of the people questioned preferred Brand X?

   _____ people preferred Brand X.

1.
2.
3.
4.
5.
6.
7.

Lesson 5 Percent of a Number

Study how decimals are used to find a percent of a number.

$$34\% \text{ of } 62.3 \dashrightarrow 62.3$$
$$\times 0.34$$
$$\overline{2492}$$
$$18690$$
$$\overline{21.182}$$

$34\% \text{ of } 62.3 = \underline{\ 21.182\ }$

Complete the following.

	a	*b*
1.	28% of 62.5 = _____	7.5% of 34 = _____
2.	73% of 95 = _____	5.5% of 9.6 = _____
3.	9.5% of 780 = _____	2% of 73.6 = _____
4.	5% of 8.5 = _____	39% of 420 = _____
5.	6.25% of 700 = _____	125% of 62.5 = _____
6.	85% of 672 = _____	7% of 86.4 = _____
7.	9% of 960 = _____	10% of 95.6 = _____
8.	140% of 280 = _____	8.5% of 785 = _____
9.	25% of 386 = _____	18% of 70 = _____
10.	67% of 18.5 = _____	7.75% of 62.4 = _____
11.	107% of 600 = _____	8% of 420 = _____
12.	83% of 840 = _____	106% of 780 = _____

Problem Solving

Solve each problem.

1. During the sale Mr. Hansen purchased a coat for 60% off the regular price. The coat normally sold for $220. How much money did he save by buying the coat on sale?

He saved $ _____.

1.

2. Mrs. James purchased a pair of gloves for 50% off of the regular price of $12.50. How much did she pay for the gloves?

She paid $ _____.

2.

3. During the sale, ladies' coats are selling for 75% of the original price. The original price is $98. What is the sale price of the coats?

The sale price is _____.

3.

4. A sales tax of 5% is charged on all purchases. What is the sales tax on a purchase of $78?

The sales tax is _____.

4.

5. Charge-account customers must pay a finance charge of 21% of their unpaid balance. What is the finance charge to a customer who has an unpaid balance of $82?

The finance charge is _____.

5.

CHAPTER 11 TEST

Complete the following. Write each fraction in simplest form.

	fraction	decimal	percent
1.	$\frac{3}{100}$	_____	_____
2.	$\frac{1}{4}$	_____	_____
3.	$\frac{7}{20}$	_____	_____
4.	_____	0.06	_____
5.	_____	0.39	_____
6.	_____	0.125	_____
7.	_____	_____	5%
8.	_____	_____	28%
9.	_____	_____	75%
10.	_____	_____	90%

Complete the following.

11.   25% of 64 = _____

12.   80% of 78 = _____

13. 6.25% of 700 = _____

14. 32.5% of 62.4 = _____

15. 8.5% of 96.8 = _____

PRE-TEST—Geometry

Match each figure with its name. You will not use all of the letters.

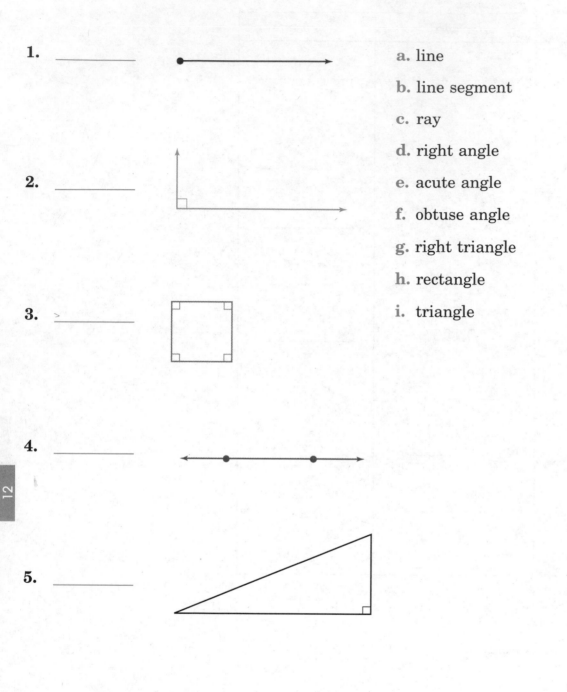

1. _____

2. _____

3. _____

4. _____

5. _____

6. _____

a. line

b. line segment

c. ray

d. right angle

e. acute angle

f. obtuse angle

g. right triangle

h. rectangle

i. triangle

Lesson 1   Lines, Line Segments, and Rays

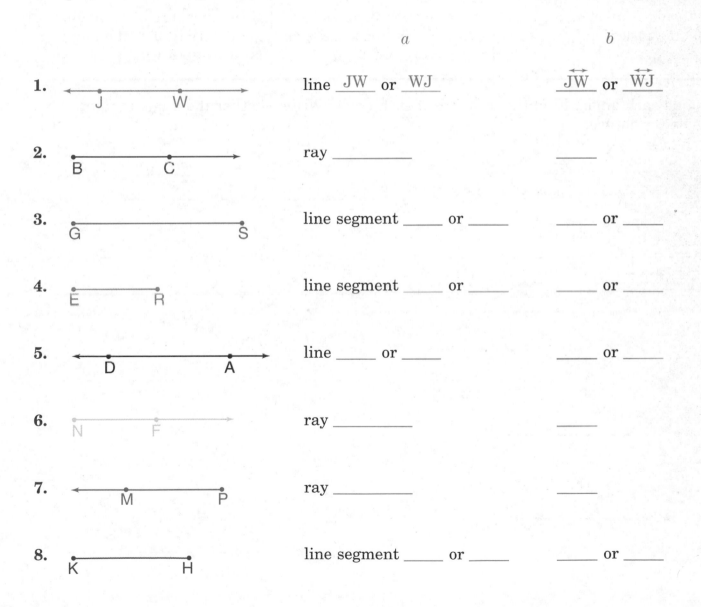

Line AB (denoted $\overleftrightarrow{AB}$) names the line that passes through points A and B. Notice that $\overleftrightarrow{AB}$ and $\overleftrightarrow{BA}$ name the same line.

Line segment CD (denoted $\overline{CD}$) consists of points C and D and all points on the line between C and D. Notice that $\overline{CD}$ and $\overline{DC}$ name the same line segment.

Ray EF (denoted $\overrightarrow{EF}$) consists of point E and all points of $\overleftrightarrow{EF}$ that are on the same side of E as F. Notice that $\overrightarrow{EF}$ and $\overrightarrow{FE}$ do **not** name the same ray.

Complete the following as shown.

a   *b*

1. line __JW__ or __WJ__ $\overleftrightarrow{JW}$ or $\overleftrightarrow{WJ}$

2. ray _____   _____

3. line segment _____ or _____   _____ or _____

4. line segment _____ or _____   _____ or _____

5. line _____ or _____   _____ or _____

6. ray _____   _____

7. ray _____   _____

8. line segment _____ or _____   _____ or _____

Lesson 2   Angles

An **angle** is formed by two rays that have a common endpoint. Angle RTS (denoted ∠RTS) is formed by ray TR and ray TS.

Does ∠STR name the same angle as ∠RTS? _____

You can find the measure of an angle with a protractor.

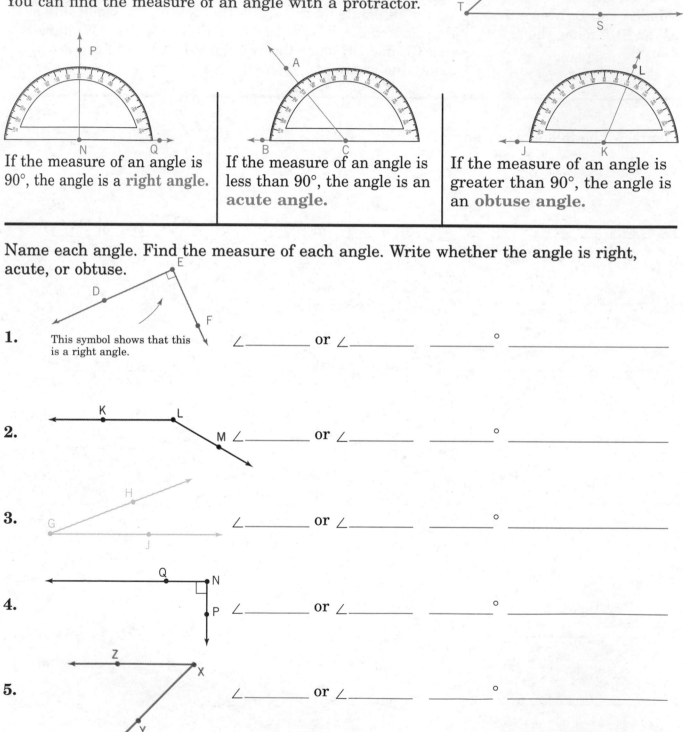

If the measure of an angle is 90°, the angle is a **right angle**.

If the measure of an angle is less than 90°, the angle is an **acute angle**.

If the measure of an angle is greater than 90°, the angle is an **obtuse angle**.

Name each angle. Find the measure of each angle. Write whether the angle is right, acute, or obtuse.

1. This symbol shows that this is a right angle. ∠_____ or ∠_____   _____° _____

2. ∠_____ or ∠_____   _____° _____

3. ∠_____ or ∠_____   _____° _____

4. ∠_____ or ∠_____   _____° _____

5. ∠_____ or ∠_____   _____° _____

140

Lesson 3 Triangles and Quadrilaterals

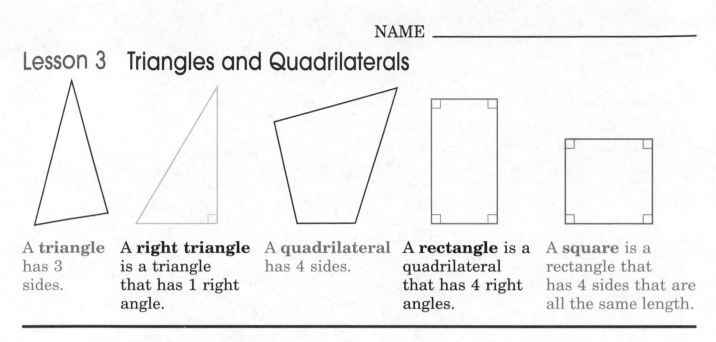

A **triangle** has 3 sides.

A **right triangle** is a triangle that has 1 right angle.

A **quadrilateral** has 4 sides.

A **rectangle** is a quadrilateral that has 4 right angles.

A **square** is a rectangle that has 4 sides that are all the same length.

Use the figures below to answer each question. You may use some letters more than once. You may not use all of the letters.

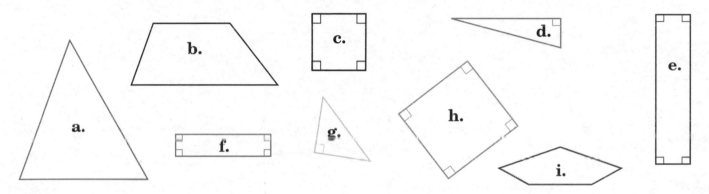

1. Which figures are triangles?

2. Which figures are right triangles? _____

3. Which figures are quadrilaterals? _____

4. Which figures are rectangles? _____

5. Which figures are squares? _____

6. Which figures are triangles, but not right triangles? _____

7. Which figures are quadrilaterals, but are not rectangles? _____

CHAPTER 12 TEST

Match each figure with its name. You will not use all of the letters.

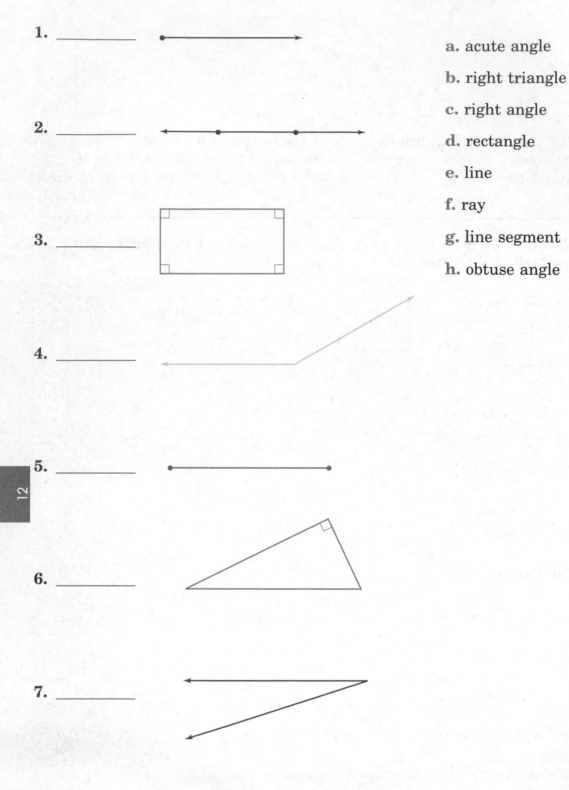

1. _____

2. _____

3. _____

4. _____

5. _____

6. _____

7. _____

a. acute angle

b. right triangle

c. right angle

d. rectangle

e. line

f. ray

g. line segment

h. obtuse angle

TEST—Chapters 1-6

Complete as indicated.

	a	*b*	*c*	*d*	*e*
1.	4 3 8 +6 2 9	8 2 5 6 4 7 9 5 5 +9 0 6 5 1	4 2 6 5 −3 0 5 1	3 7 1 2 8 −1 8 0 6 7	9 7 8 2 4 −8 6 9 8 7
2.	2 1 7 ×8	1 3 4 8 ×6	2 3 4 ×7 5	6 9 5 4 ×9 1 4	8 2 6 1 ×8 0 3
3.	47) 5 6 4	9) 2 6 7 4 1	35) 8 2 0 6	20) 8 3 2 7 5	86) 1 7 8 2 4
4.	4.6 +7.8	0.8 6 7 0.2 4 1 +0.3 7 8	$2 7.6 5 +1 8.2 0	$1 2.6 5 −9.3 6	1 8.2 7 −9.6 5 8

Write each answer in simplest form.

	a	*b*	*c*	*d*	*e*
5.	$\frac{1}{4} \times \frac{5}{6}$	$\frac{3}{5} \times \frac{10}{21}$	$8 \times \frac{2}{3}$	$2 \times 3\frac{1}{2}$	$2\frac{6}{7} \times 1\frac{2}{5}$
6.	$\frac{4}{5}$ $+\frac{1}{5}$	$\frac{1}{2}$ $+\frac{2}{3}$	$\frac{7}{8}$ $+\frac{5}{6}$	$3\frac{1}{3}$ $+2\frac{1}{4}$	$4\frac{1}{2}$ $2\frac{2}{3}$ $+5\frac{3}{4}$

TEST—Chapters 1-6 (continued)

Complete the following so the numerals in each row name the same number.

fractions or mixed numerals	decimals		
	tenths	hundredths	thousandths
7.		2.50	
8. $4\frac{1}{10}$			

Write each answer in simplest form.

	a	*b*	*c*	*d*	*e*
9.	$\frac{6}{7}$ $-\frac{4}{7}$	$\frac{9}{10}$ $-\frac{3}{5}$	8 $-\frac{7}{8}$	$6\frac{3}{4}$ $-4\frac{1}{2}$	$5\frac{1}{3}$ $-3\frac{5}{8}$
10.	$8 \div \frac{1}{3}$	$\frac{2}{5} \div 7$	$\frac{7}{8} \div \frac{3}{4}$	$1\frac{1}{2} \div 3$	$2\frac{1}{4} \div 1\frac{1}{2}$

Solve each problem. Write each answer in simplest form.

11. A truck was carrying $\frac{3}{4}$ ton of sand. Two-thirds of the sand was used to make cement. How much sand was used to make cement?

_____ ton of sand was used to make cement.

12. Last month $1\frac{1}{2}$ inches of rain fell. This month $3\frac{1}{4}$ inches of rain fell. How much more rain fell this month than last month?

_____ inches more rain fell this month.

13. Ranita bought a purse for $27.65, a blouse for $21.89, and a pair of shoes for $58.80. The sales tax was $5.42. How much did she spend in all?

She spent $_____ in all.

14. Each sheet of metal is 0.024 centimeter thick. There are 136 sheets of metal in a stack. How high is the stack?

The stack is _____ centimeters tall.

11.

12.

13.

14.

FINAL TEST—Chapters 1-12

Complete as indicated.

	a	b	c	d	e
1.	5 6 2 7 +1 7 9 5	4 5 2 1 6 5 3 +7 6 5 9	7 1 2 5 6 1 5 2 3 4 +6 9 5 4	2 9 5 −1 7 6	6 2 4 3 −8 1 2
2.	9 0 0 6 −7 3 2 8	8 7 2 4 0 −1 5 9 6 7	1 7 8 ×9	2 6 7 ×3 8	8 7 6 5 ×2 7
3.	1 0 7 4 ×4 6 5	6) 2 9 5	8) 1 3 7 6 5	12) 4 3 8 0	78) 8 6 5 3 4
4.	6.7 +3.2 4	8.9 1 7 3.1 +1 6.2 7	0.5 0 7 +0.4 9 8 2	2 5.6 8 3.5 +7.9 2	0.8 7 −0.6
5.	2.0 7 −1.6 9 5	1 5.3 4 6 −9.2 9	0.2 1 5 ×0.6	2 4 3 ×0.6 5	7.1 5 ×1.3
6.	1.8 ×0.0 0 5	3) 1 2.4 5	0.8) 3.4	1.3) 3.1 2	0.009) 0.8 1

Write each answer in simplest form.

	a	b	c	d
7.	$\frac{1}{3} \times \frac{3}{5}$	$7 \times \frac{3}{5}$	$5\frac{1}{2} \times 4$	$3\frac{1}{5} \times 6\frac{1}{4}$

FINAL TEST (continued)

Write each answer in simplest form.

	a	b	c	d
8.	$\dfrac{7}{8}$ $+\dfrac{3}{8}$	$\dfrac{5}{6}$ $+\dfrac{2}{3}$	$3\dfrac{1}{2}$ $+4\dfrac{1}{4}$	$5\dfrac{3}{4}$ $+6\dfrac{5}{6}$
9.	$\dfrac{9}{10}$ $-\dfrac{3}{10}$	$\dfrac{5}{8}$ $-\dfrac{1}{4}$	$7\dfrac{1}{2}$ $-3\dfrac{1}{3}$	$6\dfrac{1}{8}$ $-4\dfrac{5}{6}$
10.	$9 \div \dfrac{1}{4}$	$\dfrac{7}{8} \div 6$	$\dfrac{3}{7} \div \dfrac{9}{10}$	$3\dfrac{3}{4} \div 1\dfrac{2}{3}$

Find the area of each figure.

a b

11.

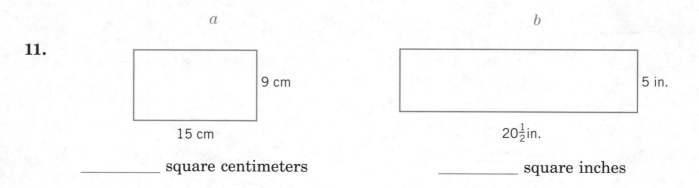

_____ square centimeters

_____ square inches

Find the volume of each figure.

a b

12.

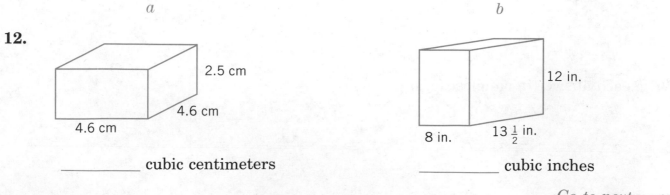

_____ cubic centimeters

_____ cubic inches

Go to next page.

Final Test (continued)

Complete the following. Write each fraction in simplest form.

	percent	fraction	decimal
13.	10%		
14.		$\frac{3}{4}$	
15.			0.5

a   b

16.   8% of 75   = _____   136% of 10.5 = _____

17.   3.2% of 800 = _____   95% of 400   = _____

Match each colored figure with its name. You will not use all the letters.

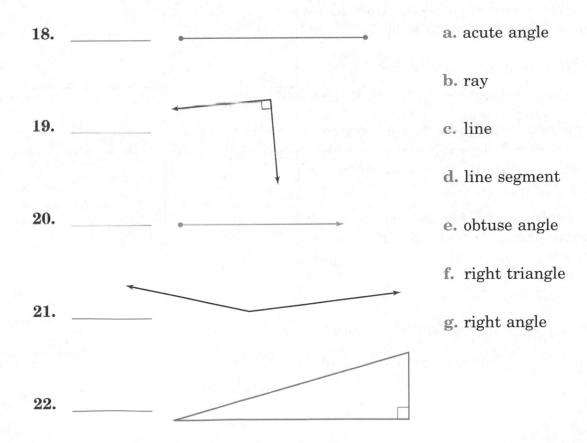

18. _____

19. _____

20. _____

21. _____

22. _____

a. acute angle

b. ray

c. line

d. line segment

e. obtuse angle

f. right triangle

g. right angle

Final Test (continued)

Complete the following.

	a	*b*
23.	2.3 m = _____ cm	235 cm = _____ mm
24.	2 kL = _____ liters	678 g = _____ kg
25.	3,520 yd = _____ mi	3 yd 4 in. = _____ in.
26.	6 cups = _____ pt	4 gal = _____ qt
27.	5 lb = _____ oz	5 hr 15 min = _____ min

Solve. Write each answer in simplest form.

28. Andrew gave the clerk a twenty-dollar bill to pay for items that totaled $15.34. How much change should he get?

He should get $ _____ in change.

29. A machine can make 382 parts each hour. The machine runs 80 hours each week. How many parts can the machine make in a week?

The machine can make _____ parts in a week.

30. Joanne can make one widget in $1\frac{1}{2}$ hours. It takes Ben $1\frac{1}{4}$ times as long to make one widget. How long does it take Ben to make one widget?

It takes _____ hours for Ben to make one widget.

31. Last month the Build-It Company made 32,626 widgets. The same number of widgets were made each day. The Build-It Company was operating 22 days last month. How many widgets were made each day?

There were _____ widgets made each day.

32. Merilynne worked the following number of hours last week: $7\frac{1}{2}$, $4\frac{3}{4}$, $8\frac{3}{4}$, $7\frac{1}{2}$, $9\frac{1}{4}$. How many hours in all did she work last week?

She worked _____ hours last week.

28.

29.

30.

31.

32.

148

Answers
Math - Grade 6
(Answers for Readiness Check, Pre-Tests and Tests are given on pages 157–159.)

Page 3

	a	b	c	d	e	f
1.	39	27	53	45	59	87
2.	59	78	78	78	69	78
3.	81	63	77	146	103	148
4.	124	151	131	111	102	152
5.	59	80	115	127	68	124
6.	186	134	109	178	180	216

Page 4

	a	b	c	d	e	f
1.	54	94	60	69	29	38
2.	43	43	54	25	10	31
3.	25	48	34	19	7	17
4.	127	156	268	107	226	59
5.	70	191	286	93	390	485
6.	87	283	376	79	437	549

Page 5

	a	b	c	d	e
1.	588	846	858	1267	1422
2.	6408	8343	9372	8733	11356
3.	78553	81378	97121	91967	91170
4.	1262	11411	12241	91272	73549
5.	60321	80121	9023	46838	53757
6.	1684	15287	13564	104566	103743
7.	42869	48277	76063	85022	79379

Page 6

1. 528 ; 746 ; 1274   4. 15342
2. 5281 ; 7390 ; 12671   5. 94400
3. 42165 ; 34895 ; 77060   6. 86889

Page 7

	a	b	c	d	e
1.	412	217	351	179	404
2.	3902	1929	4895	1889	849
3.	3031	1434	2088	2314	5048
4.	48913	39516	48917	53750	24321
5.	20937	23476	38708	34800	12200
6.	26035	23761	65995	60693	441

Page 8

1. 500 ; 385 ; 115   3. 1464   5. 36332
2. 1516 ; 842 ; 674   4. 48459   6. 13687

Page 9

	a	b	c	d	e	f
1.	38	53	58	73	139	135
2.	55	51	9	66	58	165
3.	887	965	877	661	1112	1622
4.	281	508	281	1788	1788	998
5.	8699	6840	10087	11324	11040	
6.	5114	4079	5670	3883	16809	
7.	73545	87550	75520	90417	95732	
8.	42101	48075	10244	29289	7718	
9.	99	1493	11796	88088	84788	

Page 10

1. add ; 1687   4. subtract ; 3695
2. subtract ; 427   5. add ; 61357
3. add ; 3043   6. add ; 60114

Page 13

	a	b	c	d	e	f	g	h
1.	0	0	0	0	7	6	1	5
2.	16	4	8	14	12	10	6	18
3.	27	21	15	0	3	18	12	9

Page 13 (continued)

4.	16	12	20	32	28	0	36	4
5.	40	10	35	25	20	15	5	0
6.	48	12	54	42	36	30	6	18
7.	63	49	42	0	7	35	56	28
8.	0	40	64	72	32	24	48	56
9.	27	81	72	9	18	63	54	36

Page 14

	a	b	c	d	e	f	g	h
1.	2	3	5	4	6	9	8	1
2.	9	6	7	8	4	5	2	1
3.	0	5	3	4	8	6	1	7
4.	5	2	1	3	8	6	9	4
5.	6	9	0	2	5	3	8	1
6.	5	4	7	1	2	6	9	8
7.	0	3	2	8	7	9	5	4
8.	2	0	7	9	6	4	3	5
9.	5	3	4	7	1	9	0	6

Page 15

	a	b	c	d	e
1.	96	92	246	624	570
2.	842	492	723	2505	954
3.	2349	4304	3810	6678	4257
4.	2066	9648	9516	10028	9771
5.	8868	40166	43434	32304	35415

Page 16

1. 24 ; 5 ; 120   3. 365 ; 3 ; 1095   5. 6802
2. 77 ; 7 ; 539   4. 3875   6. 20755

Page 17

	a	b	c	d	e
1.	1197	1536	4725	6480	11592
2.	14337	76820	50328	172044	651636
3.	88382	300048	90272	537536	
4.	1243380	2411010	1889280	3449412	

Page 18

1. 28 ; 35 ; 980   4. 104224
2. 47 ; 19 ; 893   5. 105264
3. 321 ; 52 ; 16692   6. 525600

Page 19

	a	b	c	d	e
1.	23	19 r1	24	19 r1	135
2.	75	98 r2	1346 r4	526 r5	709

Page 20

1. 92 ; 5 ; 18   3. 305   5. 3258
2. 258   4. 68 ; 1   6. 384 ; 3

Page 21

	a	b	c	d	e
1.	32 r10	27	45 r9	26 r25	92
2.	142 r27	346 r10	356 r49	525 r25	351

Page 22

1. 988 ; 26 ; 38   3. 309 ; 25   5. 225
2. 41 ; 3   4. 75   6. 752 ; 28

Page 23

	a	b	c	d	e
1.	245	1735	3080	12942	29436
2.	3145	2592	32844	10982	117612
3.	20856	222390	76245	526787	577382
4.	17 r12	12 r32	38	122 r4	157
5.	206 r2	63 r3	425	468 r11	1062 r17

Answers Grade 6

Page 24
1. multiply; 48750
2. divide; 7
3. multiply; 43680
4. divide; 77; 15
5. divide; 123; 10
6. multiply; 524160

Page 27

	a	b	c	d
1.	$\frac{1}{2}$	$\frac{3}{4}$	$\frac{1}{3}$	$\frac{1}{5}$
2.	$\frac{3}{5}$	$\frac{3}{8}$	$\frac{5}{6}$	$\frac{5}{8}$

	a	b
3.	$\frac{1}{2}$	$\frac{3}{8}$
4.	$\frac{2}{3}$	$\frac{4}{7}$
5.	$\frac{3}{4}$	$\frac{3}{7}$

	a	b
6.	$\frac{4}{5}$	$\frac{7}{8}$
7.	$\frac{5}{6}$	$\frac{7}{9}$
8.	$\frac{4}{7}$	$\frac{3}{5}$
9.	$\frac{5}{8}$	$\frac{2}{7}$
10.	$\frac{9}{10}$	$\frac{4}{9}$

Page 28

	a	b	c	d
1.	$\frac{1}{5}$	4	$3;\frac{3}{4}$	$9\frac{1}{3}$
2.	$\frac{2}{3}$	5	$6;\frac{2}{5}$	$8\frac{7}{8}$
3.	$\frac{1}{8}$	2	$3;\frac{1}{3}$	$5\frac{3}{7}$

	a	b	c
4.	$2\frac{1}{2}$	$1\frac{4}{5}$	$3\frac{1}{2}$
5.	$2\frac{1}{4}$	$1\frac{1}{5}$	$2\frac{2}{3}$
6.	$4\frac{2}{3}$	$3\frac{1}{3}$	$3\frac{2}{5}$

	a	b	c
7.	less than 1	greater than 1	equal to 1
8.	less than 1	equal to 1	greater than 1
9.	less than 1	greater than 1	greater than 1

Page 29

	a	b	c	d
1.	$\frac{4}{5}$	$\frac{7}{7}$	$\frac{4}{7}$	$\frac{4}{5}$
2.	$\frac{5}{6}$	$\frac{4}{7}$	$\frac{3}{8}$	$\frac{3}{4}$
3.	$\frac{7}{10}$	$\frac{5}{12}$	$\frac{9}{11}$	$\frac{11}{15}$

	a	b	c	d	e	f
4.	$\frac{5}{6}$	$\frac{7}{8}$	$\frac{3}{7}$	$\frac{9}{10}$	$\frac{11}{12}$	$\frac{4}{11}$
5.	$\frac{3}{5}$	$\frac{6}{7}$	$\frac{5}{8}$	$\frac{7}{10}$	$\frac{11}{15}$	$\frac{7}{12}$

Page 30

	a	b	c
1.	$\frac{21}{8}$	$\frac{13}{5}$	$\frac{11}{3}$
2.	$\frac{37}{10}$	$\frac{32}{3}$	$\frac{29}{2}$

	a	b	c
3.	$\frac{55}{8}$	$\frac{59}{10}$	$\frac{161}{12}$
4.	$\frac{29}{6}$	$\frac{31}{4}$	$\frac{107}{12}$

Page 31

	a	b	c	d
1.	$\frac{1}{6}$	$\frac{3}{8}$	$\frac{1}{12}$	$\frac{3}{10}$
2.	$\frac{9}{20}$	$\frac{12}{35}$	$\frac{8}{15}$	$\frac{15}{56}$
3.	$\frac{8}{15}$	$\frac{1}{16}$	$\frac{15}{28}$	$\frac{21}{40}$
4.	$\frac{18}{35}$	$\frac{2}{27}$	$\frac{15}{56}$	$\frac{6}{35}$
5.	$\frac{49}{64}$	$\frac{4}{9}$	$\frac{8}{27}$	$\frac{24}{35}$
6.	$\frac{40}{63}$	$\frac{5}{24}$	$\frac{25}{42}$	$\frac{15}{64}$

Page 32

	a	b	c	d
1.		4	8	9
2.		24	30	25
3.	8	80	10	15

Page 33
1. 1,2,3,6 / 1,2,5,10   1,2   2
2. 1,5 / 1,2,4,8   1   1
3. 1,2,3,4,6,12 / 1,3,5,15   1,3   3

Page 33 (continued)
4. 1,2,5,10 / 1,2,4,5,10,20   1,2,5,10   10
5. 1,2,7,14 / 1,2,4,8,16   1,2   2
6. 1,3,5,15 / 1,7   1   1
7. 1,2,3,4,6,8,12,24 / 1,2,3,6,9,18   1,2,3,6   6

Page 34

	a	b	c
1.	$\frac{4}{5}$	$\frac{1}{2}$	$\frac{2}{3}$
2.	$2\frac{1}{2}$	$3\frac{2}{3}$	$5\frac{4}{5}$
3.	$\frac{2}{3}$	$5\frac{3}{4}$	$\frac{5}{6}$

	a	b	c
4.	$6\frac{2}{3}$	$\frac{5}{6}$	$3\frac{3}{4}$
5.	$\frac{4}{5}$	$3\frac{7}{9}$	$\frac{1}{2}$

Page 35

	a	b	c	d
1.	$\frac{3}{10}$	$\frac{8}{15}$	$\frac{4}{9}$	$\frac{5}{42}$
2.	$\frac{3}{5}$	$\frac{5}{9}$	$\frac{4}{7}$	$\frac{4}{15}$
3.	$\frac{1}{3}$	$\frac{2}{3}$	$\frac{1}{4}$	$\frac{1}{6}$
4.	$\frac{9}{20}$	$\frac{3}{8}$	$\frac{4}{15}$	$\frac{3}{4}$
5.	$\frac{10}{21}$	$\frac{21}{80}$	$\frac{1}{2}$	$\frac{27}{35}$

Page 36
1. $\frac{3}{8}$ 3. $\frac{2}{5}$ 5. $\frac{1}{4}$ 7. $\frac{1}{6}$
2. $\frac{8}{15}$ 4. $\frac{1}{2}$ 6. $\frac{1}{3}$

Page 37

	a	b	c	d
1.	$3\frac{1}{3}$	$4\frac{4}{5}$	$4\frac{1}{2}$	$5\frac{1}{4}$
2.	$7\frac{1}{2}$	$1\frac{1}{2}$	$4\frac{1}{2}$	8
3.	$7\frac{1}{2}$	$6\frac{2}{3}$	$6\frac{4}{5}$	$18\frac{2}{3}$

Page 38
1. $2\frac{1}{4}$ 3. $10\frac{1}{2}$ 5. 3   7. 16 ; 8
2. 8   4. $9\frac{3}{8}$ 6. $1\frac{1}{2}$

Page 39

	a	b	c	d
1.	$6\frac{8}{15}$	$4\frac{1}{12}$	$4\frac{1}{6}$	$7\frac{1}{9}$
2.	$5\frac{2}{5}$	$4\frac{1}{4}$	$6\frac{2}{5}$	$3\frac{1}{5}$

	a	b	c	d
3.	$8\frac{3}{4}$	$6\frac{3}{8}$	$5\frac{1}{4}$	$12\frac{1}{2}$
4.	$32\frac{15}{16}$	$6\frac{1}{2}$	$1\frac{9}{16}$	$20\frac{5}{6}$

Page 40
1. $3\frac{5}{9}$ 3. $31\frac{7}{8}$ 5. $15\frac{3}{4}$ 7. 26   9. $3\frac{3}{4}$
2. 6   4. $4\frac{1}{12}$ 6. $25\frac{1}{3}$ 8. $5\frac{1}{4}$

Page 43

	a	b	c	d	e
1.	$\frac{3}{5}$	$\frac{6}{7}$	$1\frac{1}{4}$	$1\frac{1}{2}$	$1\frac{3}{4}$
2.	$\frac{1}{6}$	$\frac{1}{2}$	$\frac{3}{7}$	$\frac{5}{9}$	$\frac{1}{2}$
3.	$\frac{9}{10}$	$1\frac{1}{3}$	$\frac{3}{4}$	$\frac{5}{6}$	$1\frac{3}{5}$
4.	$\frac{2}{3}$	$\frac{5}{8}$	$\frac{1}{3}$	$\frac{1}{2}$	$\frac{3}{8}$
5.	$1\frac{1}{4}$	$\frac{1}{3}$	$1\frac{1}{5}$	$\frac{2}{5}$	$\frac{6}{7}$

Page 44
1. $\frac{1}{2}$ 3. $\frac{3}{4}$ 5. $\frac{1}{6}$ 7. 1
2. $\frac{1}{2}$ 4. $\frac{5}{8}$ 6. $1\frac{1}{2}$ 8. $\frac{2}{3}$

Answers Grade 6

Page 45

	a	b	c	d		a	b	c	d
1.	$1\frac{4}{15}$	$1\frac{1}{30}$	$\frac{5}{6}$	$\frac{19}{30}$	3.	$1\frac{5}{24}$	$\frac{13}{24}$	$1\frac{3}{20}$	$\frac{1}{6}$
2.	$\frac{5}{12}$	$\frac{13}{30}$	$\frac{5}{24}$	$\frac{5}{12}$	4.	$1\frac{1}{12}$	$\frac{4}{15}$	$1\frac{3}{10}$	
2.	$\frac{1}{12}$								

Page 46

	a	b	c	d
1.	$\frac{9}{10}$	$\frac{11}{15}$	$1\frac{1}{4}$	$1\frac{1}{8}$
2.	$\frac{5}{12}$	$\frac{1}{10}$	$\frac{1}{2}$	$\frac{1}{5}$
3.	$1\frac{2}{5}$	$\frac{1}{12}$	$1\frac{1}{3}$	$\frac{1}{2}$
4.	$1\frac{1}{2}$	$\frac{2}{3}$	$1\frac{2}{15}$	$\frac{2}{5}$

Page 47

	a	b	c	d
1.	$6\frac{1}{20}$	$3\frac{11}{12}$	$7\frac{1}{8}$	$4\frac{3}{4}$
2.	$10\frac{5}{8}$	$11\frac{7}{10}$	$3\frac{13}{30}$	$4\frac{11}{15}$
3.	$8\frac{7}{12}$	$5\frac{19}{20}$	$7\frac{3}{4}$	7
4.	$4\frac{23}{30}$	$6\frac{5}{24}$	$6\frac{5}{8}$	$8\frac{17}{30}$

Page 48

	a	b	c	d
1.	$6\frac{1}{4}$	$3\frac{1}{2}$	$4\frac{1}{3}$	$7\frac{7}{8}$
2.	$2\frac{3}{10}$	$2\frac{2}{9}$	$3\frac{1}{3}$	$2\frac{1}{2}$
3.	$4\frac{2}{5}$	$1\frac{5}{8}$	$1\frac{1}{6}$	$7\frac{7}{10}$
4.	$3\frac{5}{12}$	$7\frac{3}{8}$	$7\frac{1}{2}$	$5\frac{1}{10}$

Page 49

	a	b	c	d
1.	$\frac{3}{4}$	$\frac{11}{12}$	$3\frac{11}{12}$	$1\frac{9}{10}$
2.	$6\frac{1}{2}$	$\frac{1}{2}$	$1\frac{5}{6}$	$1\frac{19}{24}$
3.	$3\frac{4}{5}$	$2\frac{1}{2}$	$6\frac{3}{4}$	$\frac{4}{5}$
4.	$1\frac{19}{20}$	$5\frac{5}{8}$	$6\frac{5}{6}$	$6\frac{5}{12}$

Page 50

1.	$\frac{3}{4}$	3.	$1\frac{1}{4}$	5.	$1\frac{1}{10}$	7.	$1\frac{7}{40}$
2.	$\frac{9}{20}$	4.	$\frac{5}{8}$	6.	$\frac{1}{10}$	8.	$\frac{23}{40}$

Page 51

	a	b	c	d
1.	$1\frac{1}{2}$	$\frac{3}{8}$	1	$2\frac{2}{3}$
2.	$1\frac{3}{8}$	$\frac{2}{15}$	$1\frac{5}{18}$	$3\frac{1}{3}$
3.	$8\frac{4}{9}$	$\frac{7}{10}$	$5\frac{1}{8}$	$8\frac{1}{4}$
4.	$4\frac{7}{15}$	$6\frac{17}{24}$	$6\frac{7}{12}$	$\frac{7}{10}$
5.	$10\frac{5}{6}$	$14\frac{3}{4}$	$10\frac{29}{120}$	$8\frac{1}{3}$

Page 52

1.	Jennifer; $\frac{1}{12}$	4.	$\frac{3}{4}$
2.	$\frac{1}{2}$	5.	$4\frac{11}{12}$
3.	$2\frac{1}{6}$	6.	$1\frac{1}{3}$

Page 55

	a	b	c	d	e	f
1.	$\frac{5}{3}$	$\frac{8}{7}$	$\frac{5}{4}$	$\frac{7}{5}$	$\frac{9}{4}$	$\frac{7}{6}$
2.	$\frac{3}{5}$	$\frac{7}{8}$	$\frac{4}{5}$	$\frac{5}{7}$	$\frac{4}{9}$	$\frac{6}{7}$
3.	8	3	4	9	16	14

Page 55 (continued)

4.	$\frac{1}{8}$	$\frac{1}{3}$	$\frac{1}{4}$	$\frac{9}{9}$	$\frac{1}{16}$	$\frac{1}{14}$
5.	$\frac{1}{8}$	$\frac{1}{3}$	$\frac{1}{4}$	$\frac{3}{9}$	$\frac{1}{16}$	$\frac{1}{14}$
6.	$\frac{5}{8}$	$\frac{1}{6}$	$\frac{1}{2}$	$\frac{6}{11}$	$\frac{4}{7}$	$\frac{1}{12}$
7.	$\frac{1}{15}$	$\frac{9}{10}$	$\frac{11}{12}$	$\frac{1}{17}$	$\frac{9}{8}$	$\frac{2}{17}$
8.	$\frac{8}{15}$	$\frac{12}{5}$	$\frac{1}{11}$	$\frac{11}{7}$	11	$\frac{3}{17}$
9.	$\frac{1}{10}$	$\frac{1}{13}$	17	$\frac{11}{5}$	$\frac{7}{9}$	$1\frac{1}{5}$
10.	$\frac{8}{5}$	6		$\frac{1}{7}$	$\frac{7}{12}$	$\frac{5}{2}$

Page 56

	a	b	c	d
1.	30	16	28	30
2.	49	$37\frac{1}{2}$	$42\frac{2}{3}$	$32\frac{2}{5}$
3.	54	16	34	16

Page 57

	a	b	c	d
1.	$\frac{1}{12}$	$\frac{1}{8}$	$\frac{1}{15}$	$\frac{1}{12}$
2.	$\frac{3}{20}$	$\frac{5}{16}$	$\frac{3}{16}$	$\frac{5}{18}$
3.	$\frac{1}{8}$	$\frac{1}{9}$	$\frac{1}{5}$	$\frac{1}{12}$

Page 58

1.	$\frac{1}{6}$	3.	$\frac{1}{4}$	5.	$\frac{7}{32}$
2.	$\frac{1}{8}$	4.	$\frac{1}{6}$	6.	$\frac{1}{6}$

Page 59

	a	b	c	d
1.	$\frac{2}{5}$	$\frac{2}{3}$	$\frac{1}{2}$	$\frac{2}{3}$
2.	$1\frac{1}{5}$	$\frac{6}{7}$	8	$1\frac{1}{4}$
3.	2	$\frac{1}{2}$	$2\frac{2}{9}$	$1\frac{1}{4}$

Page 60

1.	3	3.	6	5.	4	7.	5	9.	4
2.	3	4.	$4\frac{1}{2}$	6.	2	8.	2		

Page 61

	a	b	c	d		a	b	c	d
1.	12	$\frac{4}{35}$	$\frac{1}{2}$	$\frac{9}{10}$	4.	$\frac{1}{5}$	2	$1\frac{1}{4}$	$7\frac{1}{2}$
2.	$1\frac{1}{4}$	24	$\frac{1}{6}$	$\frac{3}{7}$	5.	1	$\frac{27}{28}$	21	$\frac{3}{14}$
3.	$2\frac{1}{2}$	$1\frac{1}{8}$	15	$\frac{0}{27}$					

Page 62

1.	27	3.	2	5.	$\frac{1}{8}$	7.	$\frac{1}{16}$
2.	$\frac{1}{12}$	4.	12	6.	$\frac{1}{2}$	8.	$\frac{5}{20}$

Page 63

	a	b	c	d
1.	$\frac{5}{6}$	$\frac{7}{15}$	3	$4\frac{1}{2}$
2.	$\frac{18}{35}$	$\frac{9}{20}$	$3\frac{3}{4}$	$1\frac{1}{2}$
3.	$6\frac{3}{10}$	$\frac{1}{9}$	$\frac{9}{25}$	$\frac{8}{15}$

Page 64

1.	4	3.	3	5.	9	7.	6
2.	10	4.	6	6.	4		

Answers Grade 6

Page 67

	a	b	c	d
1.	.6	.2	.8	.5
2.	4.7	5.9	18.2	423.6
3.	$\frac{7}{10}$	$\frac{3}{10}$	$\frac{1}{10}$	$\frac{9}{10}$
4.	$4\frac{9}{10}$	$12\frac{7}{10}$	$15\frac{1}{10}$	$217\frac{3}{10}$
5.	.8	3.7		
6.	.4	25.8		
7.	.5	100.6		

8. nine tenths
9. three and seven tenths
10. twenty-one and two tenths

Page 68

	a	b	c
1.	.08	.16	.05
2.	1.36	8.06	9.12
3.	12.45	43.67	26.04
4.	142.08	436.42	389.89
5.	$\frac{17}{100}$	$\frac{3}{100}$	$\frac{41}{100}$
6.	$5\frac{19}{100}$	$6\frac{47}{100}$	$5\frac{1}{100}$
7.	$21\frac{7}{100}$	$23\frac{99}{100}$	$44\frac{89}{100}$
8.	$142\frac{33}{100}$	$483\frac{3}{100}$	$185\frac{63}{100}$

	a	b
9.	.08	6.23
10.	.95	14.60
11.	.48	4.44

Page 69

1.	.008	.017	.0054
2.	.0125	.430	.0306
3.	4.004	3.0041	6.183
4.	35.0078	42.019	196.006
5.	$\frac{9}{1000}$	$\frac{19}{10000}$	$\frac{3}{10000}$
6.	$\frac{123}{1000}$	$\frac{441}{10000}$	$\frac{219}{1000}$
7.	$4\frac{11}{1000}$	$2\frac{1011}{10000}$	$6\frac{14}{10000}$
8.	$36\frac{37}{1000}$	$3\frac{433}{1000}$	$100\frac{1}{10000}$

	a	b
9.	.053	10.0009
10.	.0011	12.018
11.	.065	12.001

Page 70

	a	b	c
1.	.6	.60	.600
2.	3.5	.28	2.190

	a	b	c
3.	2.8	.35	.056
4.	2.2	.38	.352

Page 71

	a	b	c	d
1.	$\frac{3}{10}$	$\frac{1}{10}$	$\frac{2}{5}$	$\frac{1}{2}$
2.	$2\frac{7}{10}$	$3\frac{3}{10}$	$7\frac{1}{5}$	$5\frac{4}{5}$
3.	$\frac{17}{100}$	$\frac{3}{100}$	$\frac{3}{20}$	$\frac{4}{5}$
4.	$5\frac{7}{100}$	$8\frac{43}{100}$	$4\frac{1}{20}$	$2\frac{11}{25}$
5.	$\frac{3}{1000}$	$\frac{17}{1000}$	$\frac{1}{8}$	$\frac{9}{200}$
6.	$3\frac{121}{1000}$	$2\frac{987}{1000}$	$4\frac{1}{4}$	$3\frac{1}{125}$
7.	$4\frac{7}{20}$	$\frac{7}{10}$	$6\frac{1}{5}$	$1\frac{7}{1000}$
8.	$2\frac{3}{5}$	$3\frac{6}{25}$	$\frac{1}{4}$	$3\frac{1}{2}$

Page 71 (continued)

9.	$5\frac{1}{8}$	$\frac{9}{10}$	$2\frac{2}{5}$	$\frac{1}{25}$
10.	$\frac{1}{100}$	$\frac{51}{1000}$	$\frac{4}{5}$	$2\frac{19}{100}$

Page 72

	a	b	c	d
1.	.2	.35	.445	
2.	7.5	4.58	3.360	
3.	$\frac{9}{10}$	$3\frac{3}{5}$	$\frac{7}{20}$	$17\frac{3}{4}$
4.	$\frac{1}{40}$	$8\frac{89}{200}$	$24\frac{61}{100}$	$8\frac{1}{20}$
5.	$\frac{3}{5}$	.6	.60	
6.	$2\frac{7}{10}$	2.7		2.700
7.	$5\frac{2}{5}$		5.40	5.400
8.		3.5	3.50	3.500
9.	$17\frac{9}{10}$		17.90	17.900
10.	$80\frac{4}{5}$	80.8		80.800

Page 73

	a	b	c	d	e
1.	.9	1.7	12.6	32.1	52.4
2.	.77	1.24	7.94	96.81	62.21
3.	.245	1.332	4.339	5.813	43.223
4.	1.8	7.5	9.9	46.8	8.4
5.	1.00	$1.04	10.54	$41.89	$37.19
6.	.721	.696	10.620	6.329	38.114

Page 74

1. 2	3. 8	5. .218	7. 7.1
2. 1.5	4. .63	6. 3.9	8. 16

Page 75

	a	b	c	d	e
1.	1.32	1.23	1.001	1.143	.845
2.	6.058	13.14	4.116	8.333	34.43
3.	1.238	.96	2.48	1.081	.915
4.	7.122	16.837	10.944	11.461	10.104

	a	b
5.	1.71	1.166
6.	.694	.853
7.	1.201	8.024
8.	2.71	26.556

Page 76

1. 1.25	3. 1.225	5. $66.55	7. $43.50
2. 1.50 or 1.5	4. 1.175	6. $26.55	8. 5.495

Page 77

	a	b	c	d	e
1.	.4	.7	.4	.8	.3
2.	.11	.33	.05	.48	$.15
3.	.111	.289	.208	.439	.379
4.	1.4	4.6	4.9	4.9	18.3
5.	3.13	$3.82	3.69	$12.65	$3.77
6.	2.212	2.209	2.812	23.802	11.196
7.	10.4	2.48	7.13	1.955	12.388

Page 78

1. .2	3. .23	5. 2.775	7. 1.8
2. .5	4. .24	6. 2.40	

Answers Grade 6

Page 79

	a	b	c	d	e
1.	.52	2.16	2.68	3.216	.646
2.	.113	.293	4.861	2.748	.982
3.	.45	.24	5.18	4.65	7.58
4.	.591	.125	2.044	2.868	10.686
5.	.436	.085	4.408	3.788	10.536
6.	32.085	38.925	39.036	23.85	1.076
7.	37.52	318.79	1.026	78.667	89.397

Page 80

1. 1.2
2. Ms. Williams ; Mr. Karns ; 6.3
3. 36.6
4. 3.5

Page 83

	a	b	c	d	e
1.	6	.6	.06	.006	.6
2.	48	4.8	.48	.048	.48
3.	15	1.5	.15	.015	.015
4.	12	.12	.012	.012	.0012
5.	42	.42	.042	.042	.0042
6.	72	.72	.072	.072	.0072

Page 84

	a	b	c	d
1.	44.8	4.48	.448	.0448
2.	129.6	12.96	1.296	.1296
3.	8.84	.884	.0884	88.4
4.	1.924	192.4	19.24	.1924
5.	7.5	.075	.75	.0075
6.	.48	.48	.048	.0048
7.	2.19	.0219	2.19	.219

Page 85

	a	b	c	d	e
1.	3.5	.6	7.2	2.1	.8
2.	.48	.06	.21	.08	.42
3.	.32	.06	.56	.54	.15
4.	.045	.035	.064	.006	.015
5.	.0024	.0024	.0009	.0056	.0006
6.	.063	.048	.024	.032	.035
7.	.0045	.0081	.0012	.0009	.0025

Page 86

	a	b	c	d	e
1.	56.42	564.2	5642	5642	5.642
2.	1.064	10.64	106.4	.106	1064
3.	2.3	23	230	.23	.23
4.	.08	.8	8	8	80
5.	15	150	1500	1500	1.5

Page 87

	a	b	c	d	e
1.	3.44	.216	.0532	.0162	.736
2.	.0411	38.56	362.8	4.571	2.496
3.	16.05	20.24	.2836	.0842	.4527
4.	1.134	.928	.075	.2226	57.76
5.	.6545	3.528	85.33	.4464	3.9075
6.	75.888	9.2796	73.536	.8164	.5328

Page 88

1. 5.4
2. .168
3. 3
4. 21.05
5. .144
6. .192
7. 3.7996
8. 478.8
9. 411.6

Page 89

	a	b	c	d
1.	.24	.72	.0049	.040
2.	1.215	.1216	.1118	18.75
3.	7.897	1.9992	16.324	4.4469
4.	9.5742	114.552	254.904	34.4258
5.	38.5014	175.417	19.4688	45.0294

Page 90

1. 40.8
2. .336
3. 1.608
4. 206.55
5. 245.025
6. 3270
7. 7.84
8. 4.032

Page 93

	a	b	c	d	e
1.	73	7.3	.73	.073	.0073
2.	1.87	.0027	.033	1.16	4.2
3.	3.5	.042	.0027	6.1	.56

Page 94

1. .2
2. 2.3
3. .003
4. .06
5. .001
6. 18.1
7. .012
8. .0084

Page 95

	a	b	c	d
1.	180	270	510	370
2.	1800	2400	1700	3700
3.	3000	3000	4000	31000

Page 96

1. 180
2. 130
3. 13000
4. 650
5. 240
6. 1250
7. 120
8. 200
9. 320

Page 97

	a	b	c	d
1.	18	2.7	.49	92
2.	14	1.7	2.8	36
3.	4	.6	18	3.7
4.	24	70	1.5	12

Page 98

	a	b	c	d
1.	60	480	230	30
2.	800	50	270	500
3.	370	1700	340	1200
4.	65	70	200	140
5.	250	8100	830	9600

Page 99

	a	b	c		a	b	c
1.	.48	2.9	.017	4.	140	1800	280
2.	150	4000	200	5.	120	28000	1.6
3.	1.4	5300	7.9				

Page 100

1. 18
2. 1 ; .5
3. 1700
4. .65
5. 840
6. 10
7. 100

Page 101

	a	b	c	d
1.	5	60	500	500
2.	3.3	1.8	4.6	.25
3.	.58	2.7	4.2	.032
4.	3000	4.2	.073	1.2

Page 102

1. 8
2. 3 ; .7
3. 80
4. 8
5. 4
6. 5
7. 100
8. .01

Page 103

	a	b	c
1.	8.2	.12	500
2.	3.3	120	76
3.	.47	2.8	9.2

Answers Grade 6

Page 104
1. .059   4. .35   6. .10
2. .12   5. .04   7. .16
3. .14

Page 107
1–3. Have a parent or teacher check your work.
4. 7   6. 75
5. 5   7. 42
8–10. Have a parent or teacher check your work.

Page 108

	a	b	c
1.	45	4.5	.045
2.	16	1.6	.016
3.	29	2.9	.029
4.	51	5.1	.051
5.	63	6.3	.063

	a	b	c
6.	5.4	8000	.234
7.	160	9	5.8
8.	.612	4000	1.3
9.	20	750	.0345
10.	7.07	.5	46.5

Page 109

	a	b
1.	4 ; 2 ; 8	1.5 ; 1.5 ; 2.25
2.	30 ; 15 ; 450	25 ; 10 ; 250
3.	17.4	
4.	20.25	
5.	518.4	

Page 110
1. 11250   4. 8400   7. 800000
2. 27   5. 1820
3. 55.25   6. 119

Page 111

	a	b	c
1.	54	64	162
2.	18.75	894.6	.18
3.	210		
4.	124.2		
5.	614.125		
6.	232.128		

Page 112
1–2. Have a parent or teacher check your work.
3. 2.4
4. 588
5. 262.5

Page 113
1. 5000   3. 25   5. 96000
2. 24   4. 8

Page 114

	a	b
1.	7000	500
2.	.005	4.5
3.	7500	2540
4.	.6	.0075
5.	3400	.3
6.	3000	.3
7.	.0006	24000
8.	.047	750
9.	20000 ; 20	

Page 115
1. 50   3. 200   5. 210
2. 1000 4. 1000

Page 116

	a	b
1.	8000	7500
2.	4.5	.038
3.	6000	.64
4.	50	4500
5.	7	7
6.	5500	210
7.	400	.345
8.	.607	8900
9.	52000	.975
10.	50000	

Page 119

	a	b	
1.	72	5	7. 64
2.	27	4	8. 113
3.	180	4	9. 17
4.	15840	5280	10. 114
5.	15	$1\frac{1}{2}$	11. 6030
6.	10560	8800	

Page 120
1. 7   4. 51   7. 32
2. 112 5. 69   8. 59
3. 375 6. 46   9. 64

Page 121

	a	b	c		
1.	54	44	49	4. $17\frac{1}{2}$	6. $8\frac{3}{4}$
2.	$3\frac{3}{4}$	$24\frac{3}{4}$	$37\frac{1}{2}$	5. $13\frac{1}{2}$	7. $3\frac{3}{4}$
3.	36				

Page 122
1. 64   3. 231 5. 9600 7. $229\frac{1}{2}$
2. 140 4. 216 6. 100

Page 123

	a	b	c	
1.	48	91	$65\frac{1}{4}$	6. $115\frac{1}{2}$
2.	$82\frac{1}{2}$	$28\frac{1}{2}$	$56\frac{1}{4}$	7. $35\frac{3}{4}$
3.	105			8. $146\frac{1}{4}$
4.	$202\frac{1}{2}$			9. $55\frac{1}{8}$
5.	$175\frac{1}{2}$			10. $404\frac{11}{16}$

Page 124
1. 4200 3. 3072 5. 25200 7. 2592
2. 450   4. $37\frac{1}{2}$ 6. $87\frac{3}{4}$ 8. 48

Page 125

	a	b	
1.	6	4	5. 5
2.	10	5	6. 23
3.	16	$2\frac{3}{4}$	7. 5
4.	6	$7\frac{1}{2}$	8. 19
			9. 15 ; 30 ; 60

Page 126

	a	b	
1.	1152	5	7. 6500
2.	8000	3	8. 165
3.	180	2	9. 108
4.	300	6	10. 260
5.	120	6	11. 56
6.	60	86	

Answers Grade 6

Page 129

1. $\frac{1}{100}$ .01
2. $\frac{7}{100}$ .07
3. $\frac{29}{100}$ .29
4. $\frac{47}{100}$ .47
5. $\frac{53}{100}$ .53
6. $\frac{21}{100}$ .21
7. $\frac{83}{100}$ .83
8. $\frac{49}{100}$ .49
9. $\frac{61}{100}$ .61
10. $\frac{9}{100}$ .09
11. $\frac{37}{100}$ .37
12. $\frac{77}{100}$ .77
13. $\frac{91}{100}$ .91
14. $\frac{33}{100}$ .33

Page 130

	a	b	c			a	b	c
1.	$\frac{1}{4}$	$\frac{9}{20}$	$1\frac{3}{5}$	6.		20%	75%	5%
2.	$\frac{13}{20}$	$1\frac{1}{5}$	$\frac{6}{25}$	7.		214%	60%	120%
3.	$\frac{39}{50}$	$\frac{11}{20}$	$2\frac{3}{5}$	8.		90%	28%	225%
4.	$\frac{7}{10}$	$1\frac{11}{25}$	$\frac{43}{50}$	9.		160%	30%	16%
5.	$\frac{19}{20}$	$\frac{2}{5}$	$1\frac{4}{5}$	10.		35%	62%	140%

Page 131

	a	b	c
1.	.135	.37	.0625
2.	.065	.0475	.0275
3.	.07	.625	.085
4.	.325	.0875	.095
5.	.0825	.175	.0375
6.	.0075	.0725	.0175
7.	60%	52%	32.5%
8.	24.75%	80%	65%
9.	14.5%	16.75%	50%
10.	6%	.7%	6.25%
11.	7.5%	.75%	.5%
12.	90%	19%	38.5%

Page 132

1. 75%
2. $\frac{13}{20}$
3. .250
4. 80%
5. $\frac{9}{20}$
6. .615
7. 98.7%
8. 70%

Page 133

	a	b		a	b
1.	$4\frac{1}{2}$	$68\frac{29}{50}$	6.	$2\frac{71}{80}$	128
2.	16	$9\frac{9}{20}$	7.	$99\frac{3}{5}$	$1\frac{31}{50}$
3.	$13\frac{3}{5}$	$18\frac{1}{5}$	8.	$5\frac{11}{50}$	336
4.	$2\frac{2}{5}$	$7\frac{43}{50}$	9.	$5\frac{22}{25}$	225
5.	$36\frac{2}{5}$	$10\frac{1}{5}$	10.	725	$3\frac{21}{25}$

Page 134

1. 33
2. 150
3. $140
4. 10
5. $6
6. $4200
7. 3760

Page 135

	a	b		a	b
1.	17.5	2.55	7.	86.4	9.56
2.	69.35	.528	8.	392	66.725
3.	74.1	1.472	9.	96.5	12.6
4.	.425	163.8	10.	12.395	4.836
5.	43.75	78.125	11.	642	33.6
6.	571.2	6.048	12.	697.2	826.8

Page 136

1. $88
2. $6.25
3. $73.50
4. $3.90
5. $1.23

Page 139

	a	b		a	b
1.	JW or WJ	$\overleftrightarrow{JW}$ or $\overleftrightarrow{WJ}$	5.	AD or DA	$\overleftrightarrow{AD}$ or $\overleftrightarrow{DA}$
2.	BC	$\overrightarrow{BC}$	6.	NF	$\overrightarrow{NF}$
3.	GS or SG	$\overline{GS}$ or $\overline{SG}$	7.	PM	$\overline{PM}$
4.	ER or RE	$\overleftrightarrow{ER}$ or $\overleftrightarrow{RE}$	8.	KH or HK	$\overline{KH}$ or $\overline{HK}$

Page 140

	a	b	c
1.	DEF or FED	90	right
2.	KLM or MLK	120	obtuse
3.	HGJ or JGH	20	acute
4.	QNP or PNQ	90	right
5.	ZXY or YXZ	45	acute

Page 141

1. a. ; d. ; g.
2. d. ; g.
3. b. ; c. ; e. ; f. ; h.
4. c. ; e. ; f. ; h.
5. c. ; h.
6. a.
7. b.

Answers for Readiness Check, Pre-Tests and Tests for Grade 6

Page v

	a	b	c	d
1.	197	969	101373	22239
2.	231	376	18228	75867
3.	2872	6970	10350	6596
4.	24381	16416	167535	2832992
5.	1208	832	211	401
6.	78 r10	13 r23	610 r34	807 r16

Page vi

	a	b	c	d		a	b	c	d
7.	$\frac{2}{5}$	$\frac{1}{12}$	$\frac{2}{9}$	$\frac{6}{7}$	10.	$\frac{7}{9}$	$\frac{5}{9}$	$\frac{2}{3}$	$\frac{2}{3}$
8.	6	33	$\frac{5}{18}$	$2\frac{2}{15}$	11.	$6\frac{7}{12}$	$7\frac{5}{6}$	$8\frac{13}{15}$	$10\frac{7}{18}$
9.	22	81	$10\frac{1}{12}$	$2\frac{3}{4}$	12.	$\frac{7}{15}$	$\frac{1}{24}$	$3\frac{7}{8}$	$2\frac{1}{8}$
					13.	$6\frac{8}{15}$	$2\frac{1}{18}$	$3\frac{5}{8}$	$\frac{1}{2}$

Page vii

	a	b	c	d	e	f	g	h
1.	10	5	8	10	11	6	3	8
2.	9	16	2	15	7	13	6	2
3.	9	0	7	6	10	5	15	6
4.	9	4	14	1	4	14	12	11
5.	8	16	7	11	8	17	3	13
6.	12	7	12	13	13	7	15	12
7.	8	11	14	8	16	11	12	17
8.	9	14	4	12	9	11	12	5
9.	10	9	10	11	15	8	10	14
10.	13	10	6	13	11	9	18	10

Page viii

	a	b	c	d	e	f	g	h
1.	9	5	6	10	5	8	13	3
2.	11	11	10	9	6	7	3	13
3.	8	10	12	10	9	2	18	12
4.	17	6	0	15	4	8	11	14
5.	7	10	12	7	11	11	14	1
6.	11	5	10	16	2	13	14	12
7.	7	15	8	12	10	15	9	10
8.	9	11	6	6	13	9	15	13
9.	17	8	16	8	12	10	9	7
10.	12	14	8	16	11	14	9	13

Page ix

	a	b	c	d	e	f	g	h
1.	3	4	3	1	4	6	1	6
2.	9	0	9	3	2	9	6	4
3.	5	5	5	1	1	2	2	4
4.	8	4	8	4	2	7	3	5
5.	7	3	8	1	8	8	5	6
6.	9	5	6	0	2	8	8	7
7.	4	6	8	3	0	5	6	6
8.	3	4	7	3	9	9	5	7
9.	7	2	8	2	9	5	3	2
10.	9	2	4	7	7	6	7	9

Page x

	a	b	c	d	e	f	g	h
1.	3	2	4	9	2	1	5	3
2.	2	5	9	5	2	3	4	9
3.	4	3	4	5	7	3	6	6
4.	6	4	0	9	2	3	7	6
5.	9	2	1	9	7	3	4	4
6.	5	3	4	7	4	6	7	8
7.	8	8	1	8	2	2	8	1
8.	7	6	0	8	6	1	7	8
9.	6	8	5	7	0	1	9	9
10.	9	0	8	5	6	5	2	7

Page xi

	a	b	c	d	e	f	g	h
1.	14	32	0	9	15	9	14	4
2.	48	5	10	6	0	36	63	3
3.	7	30	0	28	12	0	20	0
4.	56	16	56	18	8	25	40	27
5.	24	0	27	12	32	42	10	42
6.	21	36	24	18	48	36	49	1
7.	18	15	24	30	2	12	54	35
8.	81	20	54	0	72	12	16	8
9.	18	4	35	64	8	45	24	6
10.	40	28	16	21	6	63	45	72

Page xii

	a	b	c	d	e	f	g	h
1.	12	4	20	56	35	64	6	0
2.	18	30	9	18	9	16	49	4
3.	24	72	0	6	42	3	40	54
4.	0	12	35	24	25	56	30	12
5.	63	28	18	2	45	8	28	0
6.	15	48	32	21	20	8	0	63
7.	14	6	36	18	0	36	40	10
8.	16	15	45	0	72	12	21	8
9.	48	16	42	81	24	32	36	5
10.	27	27	0	14	10	7	24	54

Page xiii

	a	b	c	d	e	f	g
1.	4	6	2	5	6	9	1
2.	1	9	7	9	4	7	3
3.	1	3	5	0	3	6	5
4.	4	8	5	8	2	6	0
5.	9	8	9	5	0	2	4
6.	6	8	1	0	7	7	5
7.	4	3	5	3	8	1	1
8.	0	2	7	6	6	2	0
9.	4	1	5	8	7	4	7
10.	2	5	9	7	8	3	7
11.	6	4	3	2	6	3	9
12.	9	8	9	4	8	2	9

Page xiv

	a	b	c	d	e	f	g
1.	2	7	3	5	0	3	9
2.	4	1	3	6	6	4	7
3.	8	9	6	4	5	8	1
4.	5	6	1	0	6	9	2
5.	5	7	7	7	4	7	1
6.	5	5	0	8	2	2	4
7.	0	4	3	8	0	5	7
8.	2	3	6	6	8	3	3
9.	3	7	6	2	3	8	1
10.	1	4	9	8	4	2	5
11.	5	7	9	9	9	2	9
12.	8	1	4	6	2	8	9

Page xv

	a	b	c	d
1.	126	45	161	659
2.	414	129 r5	683	2720
3.	316 r10	835	19296	183
4.	6815	7728	3578	71
5.	53592	13 r2	2114	4260
6.	3189	12391	325312	73

Page xvi

	a	b	c	d
7.	8113	4887	26100	13 r23
8.	359370	46264	63376	31 r8
9.	211	615994	195533	737993
10.	88777	401	3770712	797197
11.	1150405	498939	610 r34	2168100

Answers

157

Answers for Readiness Check, Pre-Tests and Tests for Grade 6

Page 1

	a	b	c	d	e	f
1.	38	50	68	95	125	122
2.	41	48	15	85	89	179
3.	769	761	975	1390	601	1520
4.	613	433	592	527	1575	2899
5.	7788	10010	10263	17190	11011	
6.	3131	1779	44298	28693	36897	
7.	85758	59473	84125	55133	81222	
8.	51123	23008	39019	55705	69676	
9.	106	1697	9542	72937	84173	

Page 2

1. 435 ; 201 ; 636   3. 759
2. 435 ; 123 ; 312

Page 11

	a	b	c	d	e
1.	51	158	154	276	631
2.	48	12	79	169	97
3.	399	7089	3686	7845	30385
4.	14313	12812	85374	53966	80097

5. subtract ; 3926   6. add ; 62842   7. 95066

Page 12

	a	b	c	d	e
1.	99	192	608	3456	2468
2.	33945	2793	15504	27082	260235
3.	39483	250560	171864	2181114	4192533
4.	9	37	17 r4	325	38
5.	147 r41	135	785	2444 r8	724 r62

Page 25

	a	b	c	d	e
1.	86	342	4056	8106	50778
2.	805	3648	5115	86352	137566
3.	43776	54825	426512	1366530	1126428
4.	4	35	14 r39	116 r24	58 r20
5.	135	27 r15	1016 r32	3844 r5	434

Page 26

	a	b	c	d
1.	$\frac{3}{10}$	$\frac{16}{35}$	$\frac{10}{21}$	$\frac{4}{25}$
2.	$\frac{1}{10}$	$\frac{5}{24}$	$\frac{9}{28}$	$\frac{4}{15}$
3.	$1\frac{1}{5}$	$4\frac{4}{9}$	$4\frac{1}{2}$	$2\frac{2}{3}$
4.	$13\frac{1}{3}$	$12\frac{1}{2}$	$\frac{2}{3}$	$10\frac{1}{2}$
5.	$2\frac{11}{12}$	$2\frac{23}{56}$	$6\frac{2}{3}$	8

Page 41

	a	b	c	d		a	b	c	d
1.	$\frac{5}{12}$	$\frac{35}{48}$	$\frac{10}{21}$	$\frac{9}{64}$	4.	$13\frac{1}{3}$	$1\frac{3}{5}$	8	$3\frac{3}{4}$
2.	$\frac{10}{21}$	$\frac{28}{45}$	$\frac{3}{4}$	$\frac{1}{2}$	5.	$3\frac{17}{21}$	$6\frac{3}{10}$	$2\frac{14}{15}$	$11\frac{2}{3}$
3.	$1\frac{1}{5}$	$4\frac{2}{7}$	4	$6\frac{2}{3}$					

Page 42

	a	b	c	d		a	b	c	d
1.	$\frac{4}{7}$	$\frac{2}{3}$	$\frac{5}{8}$	$\frac{3}{5}$	4.	$3\frac{1}{4}$	$4\frac{23}{40}$	$5\frac{1}{9}$	$1\frac{3}{4}$
2.	$1\frac{1}{6}$	$1\frac{1}{4}$	$\frac{11}{24}$	$\frac{11}{40}$	5.	$2\frac{5}{18}$	$4\frac{1}{2}$	$10\frac{7}{30}$	9
3.	$2\frac{3}{5}$	$\frac{1}{8}$	$5\frac{13}{30}$	$3\frac{9}{10}$					

Page 53

	a	b	c	d		a	b	c	d
1.	$\frac{7}{8}$	$\frac{1}{2}$	$1\frac{1}{6}$	$\frac{2}{9}$	4.	$5\frac{13}{30}$	$3\frac{11}{40}$	$5\frac{13}{24}$	$6\frac{2}{3}$
2.	$1\frac{1}{18}$	$1\frac{5}{24}$	$\frac{1}{2}$	$\frac{1}{12}$	5.	$9\frac{7}{20}$	$3\frac{1}{8}$	$12\frac{59}{120}$	$11\frac{7}{24}$
3.	$5\frac{8}{9}$	$2\frac{3}{7}$	$5\frac{5}{24}$	$3\frac{5}{8}$					

Page 54

	a	b	c	d
1.	8	$10\frac{1}{2}$	10	$10\frac{1}{2}$
2.	$\frac{1}{8}$	$\frac{3}{10}$	$\frac{1}{7}$	$\frac{4}{27}$
3.	$\frac{2}{7}$	$\frac{1}{2}$	2	$1\frac{1}{6}$
4.	$1\frac{1}{4}$	$\frac{9}{10}$	2	$1\frac{1}{3}$
5.	$\frac{3}{4}$	$2\frac{1}{2}$	$\frac{3}{14}$	$2\frac{1}{7}$

Page 65

	a	b	c	d		a	b	c	d
1.	15	$10\frac{2}{3}$	6	$11\frac{2}{3}$	4.	$1\frac{1}{2}$	$1\frac{1}{15}$	$1\frac{1}{6}$	$\frac{3}{4}$
2.	$\frac{1}{6}$	$\frac{4}{21}$	$\frac{1}{9}$	$\frac{3}{28}$	5.	$\frac{7}{15}$	$3\frac{3}{5}$	$\frac{2}{9}$	$2\frac{2}{9}$
3.	$\frac{4}{9}$	$\frac{1}{2}$	2	$1\frac{1}{3}$					

Page 66

	a	b	c	d
1.	.7	3.19	5.025	
2.	.8	3.32	3.128	
3.	$\frac{4}{5}$	$9\frac{33}{100}$	$16\frac{1}{8}$	
4.	.8	1.07	8.023	14.076
5.	1.1	.76	.438	10.274
6.	1.08	1.086	7.525	46.208
7.	.32	3.317	3.55	.285

Page 81

	a	b	c	d
1.	.175	9.4	3.08	
2.	.90	3.2	5.300	
3.	$\frac{3}{40}$	$8\frac{3}{5}$	$16\frac{49}{100}$	
4.	1.3	.95	14.361	30.646
5.	1.7	4.51	.067	5.697
6.	1.32	.415	18.273	57.355
7.	.166	2.59	2.784	4.825

Page 82

	a	b	c	d	e
1.	3.5	.8	3.6	1.2	3
2.	.42	.06	.32	.72	.4
3.	.012	.008	.006	.004	.012
4.	.21	.08	.24	.54	.4
5.	.048	.005	.006	.0042	.0004
6.	4	.8	67.2	234	5680
7.	4.8	.235	.272	1.2525	.585

Page 91

	a	b	c	d	e
1.	.48	1.26	.2772	2.226	4.844
2.	5.4	.72	29.82	.48	75.92
3.	.015	.576	2.835	35.38	14.952
4.	.08	.212	.2408	118.712	16.28
5.	.0054	.0134	37.24	15.5944	264.176

Page 92

	a	b	c	d
1.	7.3	.27	.045	.0019
2.	20	150	2100	4000
3.	1.2	21	2.4	5
4.	80	60	3630	600
5.	150	.14	.46	.92

Page 105

	a	b	c	d
1.	.023	.14	3.7	.0051
2.	1100	12000	60	2100
3.	23	1.4	2.4	7
4.	900	70	90	10300
5.	25	1.4	2.6	.073

Page 106

	a	b		a	b
1.	7000	.085	5.	3500	.0065
2.	190	.045	6.	8200	.255
3.	6000	.007	7.	289	8.5
4.	5000	4	8.	90	45

Page 117

	a	b		a	b
1.	9000	.365	6.	900	.785
2.	720	.084	7.	2000	998
3.	26000	.017	8.	1.5	450
4.	4510	.065	9.	25.2	9.8
5.	6800	3.5	10.	240	70.2

Page 118

	a	b		
1.	36	4	9. 56	
2.	18	8	10. 15	
3.	10560	5280	11. 38	
4.	6	7	12. 150	
5.	14	2		
6.	32	1		a b
7.	360	3	13.	28 18
8.	2	2	14.	330

Page 127

	a	b		a	b
1.	96	6	9.	70	48
2.	15	10	10.	17	3
3.	10560	1760			
4.	12	$5\frac{1}{2}$	11. 76		
5.	36	6	12. 210		
6.	20	2	13. 4320		
7.	96	2		a	b
8.	300	2	14.	56	45

Page 128

	a	b	
1.	7	90	
2.	35	52	
3.	7	40	
4.	13.5	135	
5.	.06	.67	
6.	.0625	1.25	
7.	$\frac{9}{100}$	$\frac{1}{5}$	
8.	$\frac{9}{20}$	$\frac{14}{25}$	
9.	.59 or $\frac{59}{100}$		7.5 or $7\frac{1}{2}$
10.	84		40.05 or $40\frac{1}{20}$
11.	36		122.01 or $122\frac{1}{100}$
12.	21.6 or $21\frac{3}{5}$		63
13.	33.75		8.194
14.	52.5		5.551

Page 137

1.	.03	3%	11.	16
2.	.25	25%	12.	62.4 or $62\frac{2}{5}$
3.	.35	35%	13.	43.75
4.	$\frac{3}{50}$	6%	14.	20.28
5.	$\frac{39}{100}$	39%	15.	8.228
6.	$\frac{1}{8}$	12.5%		
7.	$\frac{1}{20}$	.05		
8.	$\frac{7}{25}$	.28		
9.	$\frac{3}{4}$	.75		
10.	$\frac{9}{10}$	.9		

Page 138

1. c	3. h	5. g			
2. d	4. a	6. f			

Page 142

1. f	4. h	7. a
2. e	5. g	
3. d	6. b	

Page 143

	a	b	c	d	e
1.	1067	181170	1214	19061	10837
2.	1736	8088	17550	6355956	6633583
3.	12	2971 r2	234 r16	4163 r15	207 r22
4.	12.4	1.486	$45.85	$3.29	8.612
5.	$\frac{5}{24}$	$\frac{2}{7}$	$5\frac{1}{3}$	7	4
6.	1	$1\frac{1}{6}$	$1\frac{17}{24}$	$5\frac{7}{12}$	$12\frac{11}{12}$

Page 144

7.	$2\frac{1}{2}$	2.5	2.50	2.500
8.	$4\frac{1}{10}$	4.1	4.10	4.100

	a	b	c	d	e
9.	$\frac{2}{7}$	$\frac{3}{10}$	$7\frac{1}{8}$	$2\frac{1}{4}$	$1\frac{17}{24}$
10.	24	$\frac{2}{35}$	$1\frac{1}{6}$	$\frac{1}{2}$	$1\frac{1}{2}$
11.	$\frac{1}{2}$	12. $1\frac{3}{4}$			
13.	$113.76	14. 3.264			

Page 145

	a	b	c	d	e
1.	7422	9764	93444	119	5431
2.	1678	71273	1602	10146	236655
3.	499410	49 r1	1720 r5	365	1109 r32
4.	9.94	28.287	1.0052	37.1	.27
5.	.375	6.056	.129	157.95	9.295
6.	.009	4.15	4.25	2.4	90

	a	b	c	d
7.	$\frac{1}{5}$	$4\frac{1}{5}$	22	20

Page 146

	a	b	c	d
8.	$1\frac{1}{4}$	$1\frac{1}{2}$	$7\frac{3}{4}$	$12\frac{7}{12}$
9.	$\frac{3}{5}$	$\frac{3}{8}$	$4\frac{1}{6}$	$1\frac{7}{24}$
10.	36	$\frac{7}{48}$	$\frac{10}{21}$	$2\frac{1}{4}$

	a	b		a	b
11.	135	$102\frac{1}{2}$	12.	52.9	1296

Page 147

13.	$\frac{1}{10}$; .1	18.	d
14.	75% ; .75	19.	g
15.	50% ; $\frac{1}{2}$	20.	b
	a b	21.	e
16.	6 14.28	22.	f
17.	25.6 380		

Page 148

	a	b		
23.	230	2350	28.	4.66
24.	2000	.678	29.	30560
25.	2	112	30.	$1\frac{7}{8}$
26.	3	16	31.	1483
27.	80	315	32.	$37\frac{3}{4}$

Record of Test Scores

Rank	Test Pages														
	17	29	41	57	67	75	85	95	105	115	125	133	144	145-6	147-50
Excellent	50	25	25	25	25	20	25	25	25	25	29 / 25	15	19	40	60
Very Good	40	20	20	20	20	15	20	20	20	20			15	30	50
Good	30	15	15	15	15	10	15	15	15	15	20 / 15	10	10	20	40 / 30
Fair	20	10	10	10	10		10	10	10	10	10	5			20
Poor	10	5	5	5	5	5	5	5	5	5	5		5	10	10
	0	0	0	0	0	0	0	0	0	0	0	0	0	0	0

To record the score you receive on a TEST:

(1) Find the vertical scale below the page number of that TEST,
(2) on that vertical scale, draw a • at the mark which represents your score.

For example, if your score for the TEST on page 17 is "My score: 32," draw a • at the 32-mark on the first vertical scale. A score of 32 would show that your rank is "Good." You can check your progress from one test to the next by connecting the dots with a line segment.